Pints and Power

Where History, Heart and the Pint Converge

FIRST POUR PRESS

Auburn, MA

Pints and Power
Where History, Heart, and the Pint Converge
© 2025 Michael Villa

Published by **First Pour Press**, Auburn, Massachusetts

Edition: First Pour Edition
ISBN: 979-8-9938481-1-2
Publication Date: November 2025
Rights: For sale with exclusive rights in all countries (World rights).

For more information, visit
www.pintsandpower.com
Follow **@pintsandpower** on Instagram and Facebook.

Dedication

To Lisa — by my side from the very first pour,
and every step along the road.

To Elisabeth — whose own journey carried
Ireland into our home.

To my children — who remind me what matters most.

To the regulars — with stories and laughter that bind,
where friendship is poured and belonging we find.

And to all who seek welcome, in places old or new,
may a pub's open door always greet you true.

FIRST POUR
EDITION

CONTENTS

FIRST POUR EDITION

INTRODUCTION

I didn't set out to write a book about Guinness. I set out to understand why it kept showing up in my life with a weight that felt larger than the glass.

One day it was a pint poured just right in a small pub in Ballymacarbry, Co. Waterford. Another day it was a moment of stillness, surrounded by strangers in a bar in Worcester, Massachusetts, who weren't strangers for long. And eventually, it became clear that what I was drinking wasn't just stout—it was story. It was pride. It was Ireland.

This is not a history book—though history pours through its pages. It's not a guide to tasting notes or factory tours. *Pints and Power* is a memoir of sorts, but not just mine. It's a record of a journey: one that follows the shape of a glass, the pace of a proper pour, and the voices that emerged when I started listening more carefully.

Guinness is the thread. But this book is about people. About identity. About the tension between longing and belonging. And about how something as simple as a pint can carry meaning across oceans and generations.

I came to this project through a back door: by way of family, of travel, of love. My daughter moved to Ireland and made a life there. I found myself returning again and again, each time falling further into the rhythm of Irish life—not as a tourist, but as someone who felt claimed by it. And when I returned home, the Guinness in my glass tasted different. More rooted. More reverent.

As the journey unfolded, I met people who mirrored what I was feeling. Some were Irish-born. Others were Irish by memory, blood, or spirit. Many of them I met at what is now my local—Boland's Bar and Patio, a pub that feels less like a business and more like a public living room—Shuggy's place.

It became a kind of home base for this book. A place where the pint was poured with care, where music filled the corners, and where conversation ran deeper than the glass. From there and beyond, each person had a story to share— a story that, somehow, always led back to Guinness.

You'll meet them throughout these pages:

Shuggy, the Dublin-born musician-turned-publican, proud owner of Certified Perfect Pints, known for his stories and brushes with fame, who invites you into his bubble to make it your own.

Michaela, a bartender from Derry who carries both the trauma of the Troubles and the pride of her people with every glass she sets down.

Barry, a teacher, and traveler who sees Guinness as both ritual and remembrance.

Kevin, Kerry-born and Boston-bred, who cheers Irish rugby as if he never left.

Niall, a Cork-born folk singer in New York who doesn't drink anymore, but still raises a Guinness 0.0 onstage—

because *"sometimes I don't want to drink a beer, but I want to smell like I've been drinking a beer"*

Gareth, from a small town in the North of Ireland, who plays and coaches the local Fenians GAA team and carries his heritage with quiet certainty—always North, never Northern.

Scott, Scotty-no-Shoes, Barefoot Scott, math teacher, darts team member, pub philosopher, self-proclaimed craft brew snob, who never wears shoes and only drinks Guinness at Shuggy's.

Conor, a young man from Limerick who straddles two worlds: insurance by day, Fenians GAA and Guinness by night.

Ged, from Liverpool, pulse of the local Official Liverpool Supporters Club, he doesn't drink alcohol on Sunday's but is at every match day, pint of Guinness 0.0 in hand, because it's never been about the alcohol—it's about identity.

Danny, a modern Irish rock icon whose music and lineage echo the same cultural pride that runs through every proper pour.

These are not characters. These are real people who have shaped me on this journey. Real voices. And they've become part of this book because they represent something larger than any one story. They represent what it means to gather, to remember, to belong.

The chapters ahead explore everything from the perfect pour to the grief of exile, the weight of legacy, and the joy of finding home in an unexpected place. They are about what Guinness holds—not just as a drink, but as a container of memory, myth, and meaning. That Guinness has not just been a companion in the Irish legacy for a quarter of a millennium, but a constant undertow pushing and pulling the Irish diaspora around the world.

I invite you to pull up a stool. Read slowly, as if waiting for the next pint to settle. And I hope that somewhere in these pages, you hear a voice that reminds you of someone you know, someplace you've been, something you've loved—or a part of yourself you've been meaning to return to.

Sláinte.

AUTHOR'S NOTE:
A WORD ON HISTORY AND THE MODERN LENS

The Guinness we know today—global, iconic, and meticulously curated—is a product of the 20th century. Its reputation as a symbol of Irish identity, quality, and quiet defiance didn't appear overnight. It was built slowly— through industrial innovation, social investment, and, eventually, deliberate branding.

But as I wrote this book, I came to recognize that I was often seeing the past through the shape of the modern pint glass. I attributed symbolism to Arthur Guinness that may not have existed in his time. I saw the brewery's survival through the Great Hunger and revolutions as constancy, when in fact, it was quiet endurance. I heard meaning in historical moments that may only echo because we now expect them to.

This book is full of reverence—but not revision. Where myth and history meet, I've tried to mark the crossing. And where modern interpretations shine through, they are offered not as fact, but as reflections of what Guinness has come to mean to us.

In that spirit, I invite you to read not just for the facts, but for the feeling. For the story beneath the pour—and the space between the sips.

FIRST POUR EDITION

PROLOGUE: THE PINT THAT FOUND ME

"You can't buy happiness, but you can buy a pint of Guinness—and that's pretty close."
– Anonymous pub sign

I didn't grow up Irish.

Our family name isn't traced back to Kilkenny or Kerry.

My sisters and I had an Irish "Grandma" who raised my mother, but the most memorable story from her time growing up was how she swore she saw the iceberg that sank the *Titanic* when she came to America. There was no cottage in the hills. No romantic yarns about fields of green. No rainbows. No leprechauns. No real connection to Ireland as part of our family heritage.

But somehow, inexplicably—I fell in love with Ireland.

. . .

It started when my daughter moved to Cork following college after missing an opportunity to study in Ireland courtesy of COVID-19. She found a path to go anyway. She left from Boston in the summer of '22 with a one-year commitment as a volunteer working with adults with intellectual and developmental disabilities.

We visited her, of course. Walked the streets. Heard the music. Sat in the pubs. And slowly, something changed.

Ireland wasn't just a place she was falling in love with. It was a place that was changing us.

She stayed the year. Found purpose. Found love. She stayed a second year. And now, she's marrying an Irish lad and preparing to move there permanently and plant her roots in a country that, somehow, began to feel like home to all of us.

. . .

When we got back to the States from our first trip, still buzzing with that quiet Irish magic, we talked about how we wished there was someplace at home that felt like a pub in Ireland.

I read about a new bar in town—a "real Irish pub" opened by a Dubliner named Shuggy. Eventually, we took an opportunity to try it out. So, we went. I ordered a Guinness.

And something special happened. Something almost spiritual.

It wasn't just another poser pint pretending to be a Guinness. It was a real GUINNESS.

In that moment, I was transported back to Ireland. I was sure I would only ever feel this way when on the Emerald Isle. It stirred that feeling. The weight of the glass. The settling of the bubbles. The anticipation as the creamy foam approached my lips.

And I haven't been able to let that feeling go.

I didn't grow up Irish. And I'm proud of where I come from.

But there's something about Ireland, and the Irish—the way pain and beauty live side by side, how the past is never far, and how the simple act of raising a glass can feel like resistance, reverence, and reunion all at once—that stays with me.

This journey isn't just bringing me closer to Ireland. It makes me feel my own Americanness even more clearly—not in the noise of who we are now, but in the clarity of who we once hoped to be, when we stood up to empire.

And yet, the pain I've come to begin to understand through Irish voices—through Shuggy, through history, through quiet stories told in back rooms—reminds me that our own history, even at its most righteous, rarely bore the weight that Ireland carried.

This book isn't claiming identity. It's searching for meaning. Through a pint. Through a story. Through a country that endures and endears at the same time.

This is that story. A hundred percent.

Michael Villa
August 25, 2025

FIRST POUR
EDITION

1 THE WORLD KNOWS THE PINT, IRELAND KNOWS THE LEGACY

"A good pint of Guinness is worth waiting for."
– Hugh Leonard

There's hardly a country on earth where the name Guinness doesn't ring a bell. Whether you're in Tokyo, Toronto, or Timbuktu, someone's pouring a pint of that unmistakable black stout with the creamy white head. But to truly understand what Guinness means, you must go beyond the brand—and step into the heart of Dublin, into the soul of Ireland itself.

In Ireland, Guinness isn't just a beverage—it's a living memory. It's passed down in stories told over the bar. It's the first drink a father buys for his son. It's the a round offered by a daughter on her father's 60th birthday. It's the taste that reminds Irish expats of home on a rainy night in New York. The global fame of Guinness is impressive, but in Ireland, it carries a depth that can't be bottled.

There, the pint isn't just about refreshment. It's about identity. It's as Irish as the Cliffs of Moher, as enduring as the River Liffey. It's one of the rare symbols that unites generations, from old lads in quiet country pubs to new generations raising a glass in Temple Bar. And that emotional connection is exactly what gives Guinness its enduring power—not just as a brand, but as a cultural icon.

MORE THAN ONE WAY TO RAISE A GLASS

It's worth asking—why Guinness?

Why not Jameson? Or Bulmers? Or Smithwick's? Or Powers? Or tea, for that matter? All of them hold their own meaning.

Jameson has become a global ambassador for Irish whiskey—smooth, accessible, and unmistakably Irish.

Bulmers (or Magners, if you've left the country) brings its own ritual, especially in warmer months.

Powers and Redbreast speak to heritage and craftsmanship, their loyalty quiet but deep.

Smithwick's has its place on the red ale side of the spectrum, while in Cork, Murphy's and Beamish stout inspire deep, generational loyalty.

And tea—humble, steadfast tea—has been a companion to more Irish stories, sorrows, and silences than any stout ever poured.

(And that's without even mentioning the border skirmishes between Barry's and Lyons—or which biscuits are worthy of the dunk: Hobnobs, digestives, or nothing but plain Rich Tea.)

Each of them belongs. Each has its place in the Irish imagination, but Guinness is different. Not just because it's iconic, but because it is the drink that most often carries memory, identity, and presence—across generations, borders, and belief systems. It doesn't matter whether you're in Dublin or Boston or Lagos or Limerick—the image of a pint of Guinness still signals something immediate, emotional, and unspoken.

It's not the most versatile. It's not the most festive. It's not even the most potent. But it is the most recognizable, the most ritualized, and the most likely to mark a moment.

That's why this book follows the shape of a pint.

Because Guinness isn't just a drink—it's the one that most often shows up when something meaningful is happening.

MORE THAN A BREWERY—A CULTURAL INSTITUTION

When Arthur Guinness signed that now-legendary 9,000-year lease at St. James's Gate in 1759, he was laying more than the foundation of a brewery—he was planting the roots of an institution. In the centuries since, Guinness has grown into something far greater than anyone could have predicted: a symbol of stability, of pride, of Irish ingenuity.

It wasn't just the size of the brewery or the quality of the stout that earned it this place in the cultural fabric. It was how Guinness embedded itself in daily life.

The company didn't just produce beer—it produced livelihoods, built housing, created schools, and set a precedent for corporate responsibility centuries before it was fashionable.

When you walk into a pub with a Guinness sign outside, you're not just entering a place to drink—you're stepping into a space of shared identity. Pubs become sacred spaces of story, song, and solidarity, and Guinness is the common thread that flows through it all.

It doesn't matter if you are a poet or a peasant, a rebel, or a redcoat—the pint is yours.

BEER WITH A BACKBONE— NAVIGATING CENTURIES OF CHANGE

Ireland's path from colonization to independence was marked by upheaval, famine, rebellion, and resilience. While political forces shifted and social movements rose and fell, Guinness remained a constant. That consistency gave people a sense of normalcy, even as the world was changing rapidly.

And yet, Guinness wasn't just riding the waves of history— it was adapting to them, sometimes even quietly shaping them. Through the 19th and early 20th centuries, the company publicly maintained political neutrality during moments of revolution, but behind the scenes, it took a strong hand in shaping labor rights, fair wages, and employee welfare.

Even during the most unstable periods, Guinness kept people employed. It kept the economy flowing. It kept pints pouring in homes and pubs that might otherwise have grown dark. Through it all, the brewery became more than a business—it became a backbone for Irish society, quietly supporting the nation through its toughest transformations.

As the brewery at St. James Gate grew, the city around it did too. As the city infrastructure expanded new canals, quays, train lines, and lorry routes were all used to their fullest. The Guinness company prospered, and the Guinness family gave back—they repaired cathedrals, preserved green public spaces, normalized indoor plumbing, opened public swimming pools, and tore down sub-standard housing, and built new homes that reshaped Dublin and the lives of their workers.

This symbiotic relationship between Guinness, Dublin and its inhabitants remains inextricably linked to this day.

2 A BREW BORN UNDER EMPIRE

"Arthur Guinness believed in staying power.
He signed a 9,000-year lease."
– Guinness Storehouse

To reach the soul of Ireland through Guinness, you must return to where it started: a leased gate, a city under empire, and a man named Arthur whose ambition quietly challenged the order of his day.

It began with a lease.
Not a toast. Not a recipe. A lease.

The year was 1759. Ireland was chained to the British Crown. Catholics—most of the population—couldn't vote, couldn't hold public office, and certainly couldn't own land. Dublin was dazzling but divided: the city of lords and landlords above, of hunger and hardship below.

And into that landscape walked Arthur Guinness.

Thirty-four years old, a Protestant and a brewer's son from County Kildare, Arthur arrived in Dublin with vision—not just for beer, but for scale. He signed a 9,000-year lease for a disused brewery at St. James's Gate, a location that gave him access to the River Liffey and the Dublin markets.

The down payment? £100. The annual rent? £45.[1]

Why 9,000 years? No one knows for sure. But it wasn't a joke. It was a statement.

Arthur Guinness wasn't just brewing beer. He was staking a claim on permanence—a declaration in ink that this was not a venture but a legacy. And he was doing it in a city where permanence, for most Irish, was a luxury denied.

DUBLIN IN CHAINS

Dublin in the mid-18th century was a paradox. On one hand, it was the second-largest city in the British Empire after London, bustling with commerce, wealth, and culture. On the other, it was a city on colonial life support—where real power flowed not from its streets but from across the sea.

The elite—the so-called Ascendancy class—were Anglo-Irish Protestants who owned the land, ran the government, and saw themselves as culturally closer to London than to Limerick. Beneath them were the native Irish, mostly Catholic, largely impoverished, legally marginalized.

This was the world Arthur Guinness stepped into—not just to brew beer, but to build a business. He had to walk a

---

[1] Guinness Storehouse, "Discover the Story of Guinness", Guinness.com, accessed May 24, 2025, https://www.guinness-storehouse.com/en/discover/story-of-guinness

delicate line. Too Irish, and he'd be distrusted. Too English, and he'd be resented. His gift was not just in fermentation—it was in navigation.

And the path he chose was porter.

THE RIGHT BEER AT THE RIGHT TIME

In 1759, the beer world was changing. Arthur initially brewed ale but also saw the future. English porters—dark, strong, and popular among London's working class—were on the rise. He began brewing his own version, adjusting the recipe, refining the roast, and eventually creating a stronger, "stouter" version that could withstand shipping, store well, and satisfy a growing urban workforce.

Guinness wasn't the only brewer in Dublin, but he was the most ambitious. He invested in equipment, expanded production, and, most importantly, pursued quality relentlessly. As early as the 1770s, Guinness beer was being exported to England.

By the 1790s, it was pouring into Caribbean ports, colonial outposts, and British navy docks.

The Empire drank.
And Guinness delivered.

WORKERS, WELFARE, AND AN EARLY SOCIAL CONTRACT

While British landlords built mansions, Guinness built wages.

Even in the late 1700s and early 1800s, Guinness employees earned higher-than-average pay. They were given medical care. Housing support. Education stipends. These weren't favors—they were investments.

Arthur saw that if you wanted loyalty and quality, you had to treat your people with respect. His early practices became the foundation of Guinness's legendary status as a welfare pioneer—decades before the industrial revolution made such benefits common.

By the early 1800s, the Guinness brewery wasn't just a place of work. It was a lifeline.

THE EXPANSION: POWER IN EVERY POUR

Arthur Guinness died in 1803. But his sons, especially Arthur Guinness II and Benjamin, took the enterprise he'd begun and amplified it.

St. James's Gate expanded. New vats. New wings. New shipping routes. Guinness became a fixture in British colonial outposts—India, Africa, the West Indies. It flowed through army mess halls, shipping docks, and gentleman's clubs from Kolkata (Calcutta) to Cape Town.

There's a hard truth here: Guinness grew, in part, because of the reach of empire. It was sold to soldiers who enforced British control. It traveled in barrels with English tea and Irish linen. It benefitted from trade networks built on imperial dominance.

But here's the other truth: Guinness was Irish.

In a world where Irishness was seen as backward, poor, and rebellious, Guinness was a symbol of excellence. It forced the empire to recognize Irish craftsmanship. It gave the Irish something to take pride in—a product that couldn't be ignored.

Guinness was born in Ireland under English rule, but it wasn't English. It was Irish from the beginning—because Arthur was Irish, because Dublin made it, because the people who poured and drank it were Irish. But as Britain expanded its empire, it carried Guinness with it—not realizing it was also carrying a taste of Irish identity.

And in that sense, every exported pint, every imperial outpost that poured the black stuff, was an unintentional act of cultural subversion. They spread the beer, but they also spread the feeling of Ireland.

Guinness went global before Ireland could, and it made space for Irishness in places where Irish people weren't even welcome yet. That's not just history. That's irony pouring through a tap.

THE NAME ON THE GATE MEANT SOMETHING

By the 1820s, Guinness was the largest brewery in Ireland. But it wasn't just the size. It was the reputation.

Arthur Guinness had built something remarkable: a brand that meant quality, consistency, and class—without losing its working-class soul.

In a colony where Irish names were often erased or anglicized, even "Guinness" bore that mark. The name is believed to be an adaptation of "Magennis"—and when

Arthur himself was laid to rest he was carried to his final home in County Kildare on a carriage draped with a cloth bearing the older family crest.[2] Yet somehow, this softened name remained unmistakably Irish.

Embossed on barrels, etched on brass taps, it carried not just beer, but identity. The name stood for what endured, even when language and lineage were rewritten.

People didn't just drink it—they talked about it, passed it down, and began to believe that maybe, just maybe, Irish hands could shape the future, not just suffer the past.

That future, in the early decades of the nineteenth century, included an unlikely common cause. Daniel O'Connell, the Liberator, was pressing for Catholic emancipation—fighting for the right of Catholics to sit in Parliament and fully participate in public life.

Arthur Guinness II was now head of the family and the business. Though he was a Protestant, he saw the justice in it. Many of his workers were Catholic. Their loyalty and skill were part of the brewery's strength, and Arthur II's own paternal style of management included tangible support for them. At this time, Guinness and O'Connell shared the same belief that Ireland would be stronger when more of its people were allowed a voice.

---

[2] Bill Yenne, *Guinness: The 250-Year Quest for the Perfect Pint* (Hoboken, NJ: John Wiley & Sons, 2007), 24.

When Catholic emancipation passed in 1829, Arthur spoke publicly and said:

> *I am much joyed at the final adjustment of the*
> *'Catholic Question'... although always a sincere*
> *advocate for Catholic freedom, I never could look my*
> *Catholic neighbour confidently in the face. I felt that I*
> *was placed in an unjust, unnatural elevation above*
> *him...*[3]

But alliances in Dublin could be fragile. The politics of the 1830s and '40s were volatile, full of factional splits and pressure from the British establishment. During that time, as O'Connell became more liberal in his push towards a Republic, Arthur II put his name to a petition against O'Connell—aligning himself with Protestant interests wary of O'Connell's broader ambitions.

It was a choice that landed like a blow. The Catholic community, including many inside the brewery gates, took it as a betrayal. The backlash was sharp and personal.

Benjamin Lee Guinness, already stepping into leadership, saw it all: the sudden shift from shared cause to open wound, the way a political signature could ripple through a workforce, a customer base, and a city. The lesson was clear—aligning Guinness too visibly with one side in

---

[3] Michele Guinness, *The Guinness Legend: The Changing Fortunes of a Great Family* (London: Hodder & Stoughton, 1989), 38.

Ireland's great divides could put the whole enterprise at risk.

It was a lesson he carried into the coming years.

THE SILENCE OF THE PINT

Between 1845 and 1852, Ireland starved.

Not from drought. Not from war.
From a system designed to survive without its people.

While the potato blight swept through the country's poorest regions, exports of grain, butter, and beef continued—shipped out from Irish ports to feed the rest of the Empire. Over a million died. More than a million more fled. Entire counties emptied.

And in Dublin, Guinness kept brewing. In fact, in 1845 production rose by 20% - a growth contributed to by the population increase in Dublin that coincided with the start of the Great Hunger.[4]

The brewery didn't cause famine. But it didn't rise to meet it either. Michele Guinness records that Arthur II, in his late seventies, read reports from England with horror. While away in the English seaside town of Torquay in March 1847,

---

[4] Edward J. Bourke, *The Guinness Story: The Family. The Business. The Black Stuff* (Dublin: The O'Brien Press Ltd, 2016), 29.

on his seventy-ninth birthday, he wrote to his son Benjamin Lee:

> *How awful do the accounts from Ireland continue and how evident is it that the exertions of the Government need to be aided by those of private individuals... You know my dear Ben that my purse is open to the call.*

It was a nudge, not an order. But the son had learned the risks of being seen to choose sides in a Catholic crisis. The O'Connell backlash was still in living memory. And the English government's own obstruction often smothered relief before it could reach the starving. In May, Arthur wrote again, wishing for *"a fair honest movement independent of party spirit,"* certain that *"if there were, I know our Firm would stand forward."*[5]

I am not yet to find record of major public efforts from the company—no massive donations, no suspension of business as usual. It wasn't alone in its silence. Most institutions failed the moment.

The famine didn't just expose a failure of agriculture. It exposed a failure of empathy, of access, of class. This wasn't a famine in the natural sense. It was a famine of permission—of who was allowed to eat and who wasn't.

And Guinness, stable and growing, stood in the center of it all. Neither worsening the crisis nor publicly relieving it, it

---

[5] Michele Guinness, *The Guinness Legend,,* 44–46.

endured quietly—in the narrow space between a father's conscience and a son's caution.

That endurance would later become part of the brand's mythology—resilience, constancy, pride. But in this chapter of history, the story is simpler. Guinness survived.

Ireland did not.

LEGACY OF RESISTANCE BY EXAMPLE

Arthur Guinness never fired a shot in a rebellion. He never signed a manifesto. But in a world built to keep Ireland small, he built something permanent.

That 9,000-year lease was not just legal—it was poetic.

It said: We're not going anywhere.
Not for 50 years. Not for 500.
This brewery, this name, this Irish creation—it stays.

And that act of quiet permanence may have done more to preserve Irish pride than any pamphlet or protest.

THE POUR

Today, Guinness Draught is the most iconic expression of the pint—it's the most theatrical. It's brewed for performance. Its unique nitrogenation gives it that signature surge and settle, a visual heartbeat in the glass. It's softer than traditional carbonation, delivering a creamy mouthfeel and tight head that doesn't scream foam but settles into silence.

Originally developed in the mid-20th century to make Guinness more accessible on draught and in cans, the nitrogen-poured pint took off. It's now the face of the brand in pubs around the world—and the one most often referenced in this book.

There are other versions of Guinness, of course. But this is the ritual pour. This is the one you wait for.

3 BREWING THROUGH REVOLUTION

"Guinness kept pouring when the city stopped speaking."
– Dublin oral history

The pint endured while the nation emptied. And as Ireland rose again through resistance, Guinness remained—not as a fighter, but as a fixture—present in the background of a revolution that reshaped the country's soul.

Ireland's revolutions didn't begin in 1916. They began long before that—before the proclamations and the bulletins, before the poets with rifles and the martyrs in uniform. The Irish story is one of centuries of conflict, a slow burn of rebellion fought not always with guns, but with songs, with stories, with memory.

On this island, land was the prize—but the Irish were the spoils. Time and again, they were conquered, cleared, dispossessed, and displaced. From Cromwell's plantations to the Penal Laws, from famine to forced emigration, the Irish were taught that their home wasn't theirs, their language was a liability, and their names could be traded for survival.

And yet, they remained. They adapted. They endured.

By the time the 20th century arrived, revolution was not a new spark—it was a smoldering inheritance. It lived in the soil, in the songs, and in the pints passed across pub counters. The Easter Rising may have brought the dream into daylight, but the struggle was always there, like a bass note under the surface of the national soul.

And into that story came Guinness. Not from the beginning, but in time to witness Ireland's modern upheavals. Brewing in the capital. Employing Catholic and Protestant alike. Watching the city change around it. Never neutral, never overtly radical—but deeply embedded, unmistakably Irish, and still standing when the smoke cleared.

BREWING NEUTRALITY IN A POLITICAL STORM

The late 18th century was not kind to Ireland. In 1798, the United Irishmen Rebellion sought to overthrow British rule and establish an independent Irish republic. Inspired by the American and French revolutions, Irish nationalists—both Protestant and Catholic—rose up.

The rebellion was crushed. What followed was the passing of the Act of Union which brought the end of 17 years of pseudo-self-rule, the abolishment of the Irish Parliament, and the birth of the United Kingdom of Great Britain and Ireland. King George III ignored plans for Catholic emancipation and again, the British hold over the Irish was tightened.[6]

Arthur Guinness doubled down and worked with his sons and was guiding the family's brewery in the heart of British-controlled Dublin to keep the business running. He didn't take sides publicly. He didn't close his gates. He didn't hang banners.

The Guinness's neutrality was not apathy—it was strategy. A strategy that saw the creation of West Indies Porter, forerunner to today's Foreign Extra Stout and growing expansion to far away ports.

Guinness believed in stability. In law and order. In economic sustainability. And while Arthur was no revolutionary, his success empowered an army of thousands of Irish workers—Catholics and Protestants alike—giving them employment, income, and most valuable of all, a degree of dignity that was rare for the time.

By the time of his father's death, the Second Arthur had already been in the business for over a decade, a time which saw the expansion of the brewery, the decision to stop brewing ale and the sales more than doubling. As the second Head Brewer of the family business, Arthur II would shepherd the company through what would become very complicated times.

---

[6] Yenne, *Guinness: The 250-Year Quest for the Perfect Pint*, 22-25-.

LABOR UNREST AND BREWING LOYALTY

Guinness's real battle wasn't with rebels—it was with labor unrest.

The 1910s and 1920s were a hotbed of strikes in Ireland. Workers demanded fair wages, housing, and safety. Guinness, already seen as a welfare pioneer, faced rising pressure to do more.

But here's what made Guinness different—workers had a pension fund, they had healthcare provided by medical staff on site at the St. James's Gate, they had paid holidays and wages were significantly higher than many of their fellow Irish workers.

When the Dublin Lockout of 1913 paralyzed the city, most Guinness workers stayed on the job. They didn't have to strike—they were already treated better than most.

Hindsight in light of the many benevolent causes and investments by the Guinness Family would characterize these efforts altruistically, however many of these ideas went further back, all the way to Arthur Guinness who simply applied good business sense to many of his decisions.

Whatever the motivation, by the time independence arrived, Guinness had built not just a workforce—but a loyal class. In a country of unrest, Guinness offered structure.

THE GREAT WAR, 1914–1919.

Guinness had been actively expanding at the turn of the century, making inroads into the beer-centric culture of Belgium, and establishing a growing presence across North America. But when Archduke Franz Ferdinand of Austria-Hungary was assassinated in 1914, the ripple effect was felt across the world. Great Britain entered the war after Germany invaded neutral Belgium, and the impact on trade was immediate.

Shipping vessels once used to transport beer across the Atlantic were commandeered for military use. Even Guinness's own private fleet was pressed into wartime service—some ships were lost to German U-boats. At home, higher taxes on alcohol—used to help fund the war—made beer more expensive and less accessible. Plans to open a second brewery in Manchester were scrapped.

Wartime strains were felt across the company. Guinness guaranteed jobs for any employee who joined the British Army, even paying half-salaries while they were away. More than 500 workers—over a fifth of the company's workforce—enlisted before the war ended.

Barley became scarce as agricultural land was redirected toward wheat to feed a nation at war. Supply chains were strained, production slowed, and familiar rituals were interrupted.

Amid this backdrop of global conflict, tensions continued to simmer at home. And for many in Ireland, the time had come to demand independence.

DUBLIN, EASTER MONDAY, 1916.

Smoke curled above the General Post Office. Bullets cracked through alleyways. Rebels armed with rifles—and poetry—had declared an Irish Republic. Dublin was in chaos. British forces struck back with ferocity. Blood on the cobblestones.

And in the middle of it all stood the city's most famous brewery. Rebel commanders had hoped to hold key strategic positions—including the area surrounding Guinness. But the Rising, despite its courage, unfolded under grim odds.

Communications broke down. A shipment of German arms was intercepted before it could land. And most fatefully, Eoin MacNeill's last-minute order telling Volunteers to stand down left Dublin's ranks thinned and fractured.

Yet on Friday, April 28th, in what would be his final dispatch, James Connolly listed the positions *"still holding their own"*: St. Stephen's Green, the Gas Works, the railway works—and this:

> *Commandant Kent (Ceannt) held the South Dublin Union and Guinness's buildings in Marrowbone Lane, and controlled James Street and district. On two occasions the enemy effected a lodgement [there] and were driven out with great loss.*[7]

---

[7] Charles Duff, *Six Days to Shake an Empire* (Cranbury, NJ: A. S. Barnes and Co., Inc., 1966), 165–67.

The factual accuracy of that report is deeply questionable. The Rising was faltering, its leaders cornered, and its outposts crumbling. Connolly's account also claimed that police barracks in North County had been held, that Northern railway telegraph lines were destroyed, and that the fight extended into counties as far-flung as Galway, Kerry, Wicklow, Wexford, and Cork.

These were not updates. They were just another act of defiance.

The dispatch wasn't meant to inform—it was meant to inspire. It was less a battle map than a morale strategy.

And the decision to name Guinness alongside sites like the GPO and St. Stephen's Green wasn't incidental. It was symbolic.

One can apply a sense of modern thinking that Guinness was more than a landmark—it was a symbol of labor, industry, Irish permanence. To say it had been defended is to suggest that Ireland itself—its dignity, its future—is still standing. However, it was more likely simply a strategic marker on the map with access to the River Liffey, the canals, part of the industrial and trade area of Dublin.

So while the bullets flew and the rebellion teetered, the brewery stood. Quiet. Closed. Enduring.

A century later, the echoes of James Connolly's final dispatch still stir—not just in textbooks or monuments, but in quiet songs and shared rituals.

One of those voices belongs to Niall Connolly—the Cork-born folk singer I introduced earlier, who I first encountered at Boland's. Niall had been invited to carry Connolly's memory in a much more deliberate way.

In 2016, on the hundredth anniversary of Connolly's execution, Niall was commissioned by Grammy-winning artist Susan McKeown to write a commemorative song for the *Cuala NYC* festival.[8] She pointed him toward an archival interview with Connolly's daughter, Nora—a deeply personal recollection that transcended the historical narrative we were all taught in school. From it came *May 12th, 1916 (A Song for James Connolly)*, a song that does not shout or march, but instead mourns—quietly, precisely, beautifully.

Niall performed the song first at Cooper Union in New York—the very hall where James Connolly himself had once stood to speak. The room that night was filled with scholars, activists, and members of the diaspora. Later that year, he performed it again with Glen Hansard at Coughlan's in Cork[9], and once more atop Apollo House in Dublin as part of

---

[8] Niall Connolly, *May 12th, 1916 (A Song for James Connolly)*, Bandcamp. https://niallconnolly.bandcamp.com/track/may-12th-1916-a-song-for-james-connolly

[9] Niall Connolly and Glen Hansard, "May 12th, 1916 – A Song for James Connolly (Live @ Coughlan's, Cork)," YouTube video, 8:17, posted by Andy Wilson, December 20, 2016 https://www.youtube.com/watch?v=vbz74mGciXU.

the *Home Sweet Home* movement[10]—a protest rooted in the very kind of social justice Connolly had long championed.

The studio version features Hansard's additional vocal and a luminous Spanish laud accompaniment by Javier Más, the longtime musical partner of Leonard Cohen[11]. The result is not a ballad of triumph, but a reflection—on sacrifice, fatherhood, failure, and the quiet resolve to stand for something even when the standing costs everything.

I've seen Niall perform in that same back room of Coughlan's where the recording with Hansard was born. It's not a stage so much as an altar—a sacred music space. Small, close, stripped of pretense. The kind of place where a song like *May 12th, 1916* doesn't just play—it lands. To hear it there, or even to imagine it in that room, is to feel history pulled taut and personal. Connolly doesn't appear as a statue or a slogan. He appears as a father. A firebrand. A man carried on a stretcher to his death.

And it brings us back to the dispatch. To that list of outposts *"holding their own"* in the final hours of the Rising—St. Stephen's Green. The Gas Works. The railway. Marrowbone Lane. And Guinness.

---

[10] Home Sweet Home was a 2016 grassroots movement in Ireland focused on housing rights. Connolly performed the song at Apollo House, a symbolic site occupied in protest of homelessness.
[11] Studio credits for *May 12th, 1916* include Glen Hansard (vocals) and Javier Más (Spanish laud), both noted on the official Bandcamp page.

The accuracy of Connolly's report is debatable. But its intent is not. These were not just strategic sites. They were symbolic pillars—anchors of morale, meaning, and myth.

Connolly knew that to include Guinness was to invoke more than a building. It was to summon Irish labor. Irish permanence. Irish dignity. To say the brewery stood was to say *Ireland still stood.*

The Rising would fall. But the story would stand.

And so the question lingers:

What role did Guinness play in Ireland's revolution?

None.

And everything.

NEUTRAL ON THE SURFACE, ESSENTIAL UNDERNEATH

Guinness took no public side in the revolution. No flags. No proclamations. No donations to the rebels or the Crown. And that silence spoke volumes.

To the British, Guinness was a loyal economic engine. To the Irish, it was a source of employment, dignity, and pride—a place where thousands of workers earned honest pay in a city built on poverty.

By 1916, Guinness employed over 3,000 people—most of them Irish Catholics. In the end, forty-three Guinness workers were imprisoned or deported for participation in the uprising. A total of eighty-five were marked absent during those days. And any employee associated with the

Irish Volunteers was summarily dismissed.[12] Guinness might not have made a public stand, but in order to survive they followed the rule of law—the rule of the English.

They couldn't afford to shut down or pick a side. And so, while the Republic was proclaimed, and the GPO burned, the brewery waited. And watched. And survived.

THE PINT AND THE PEOPLE

After the rebellion was crushed, and the leaders executed, the city mourned. But it also gathered.

And where did it gather? In the pubs.

It's in those dim corners of Irish pubs—between grief and courage—that Guinness quietly became a source of stability. Not through speeches, but through the pour. The ritual. The pause.

A Guinness was something you could count on in a world unraveling. It was poured in silence. Raised in memory, and sipped while stories turned into songs.

THE WAR OF INDEPENDENCE, 1919–1921

The Easter Rising lit a fuse. Within three years, Ireland launched a full-scale guerrilla war against British rule. Michael Collins and the Irish Republican Army (IRA) used

---

[12] Bourke *The Guinness Story: The Family. The Business. The Black Stuff*, 154-155.

ambushes, intelligence, and propaganda to destabilize British control.

Guinness still stayed quiet. And still, it poured.

Michael Collins was a man of shadows and secrets, yet the pint was never far from him. During the War of Independence, Guinness was present in the safe houses where his men gathered, in the pubs where information passed, in the glasses raised after missions survived.

Collins understood the pub not only as a social space but as a shield. A pint in hand made a rebel look like a regular. A round bought on credit could mean loyalty pledged to the cause. Guinness, in those moments, was more than a drink. It was camouflage.

There are stories—some apocryphal, some true—of Collins slipping into a bar, nodding to the bartender, and blending seamlessly into the hum of a Dublin night. The pint beside him was both cover and comfort. In those dangerous years, it became part of the ordinary, extraordinary rhythm of rebellion.

Several Dublin pubs—like J&M Cleary's and Devlin's—are recorded as covert hubs where Collins and his circle met, proof that the pint and the pub were inseparable from the work of revolution. Devlin's was marked with a heritage plaque by the Dublin City Council in 2024. The council explained the importance of the location.

> *Meetings were held daily at the pub, attended by Michael Collins, Frank Thornton, Liam Tobin, Emmet Dalton and many others of the leadership of the*

Volunteers and the IRB... As many as eight to ten volunteers and officers were accommodated there every night during this period. Devlin was himself an Intelligence Officer and was entrusted with the safe keeping of National Loan Funds.[13]

Through boycotts, blacklists, rationing, and raids, Guinness maintained operations. It worked with British trade networks—but remained deeply Irish. In some rebel areas, IRA leaders protected Guinness shipments, recognizing the brewery's importance to working-class families.

The pint became a strange kind of truce.
It flowed across enemy lines.
It offered respite—if not peace.

THE CIVIL WAR (1922–1923): BROTHERS AND BARRELS

After the Anglo-Irish Treaty was signed, and the Free State formed, civil war broke out between pro- and anti-Treaty forces. Families were split. Friends turned on each other. The nation continued to bleed.

And yet—Guinness brewed on.

During the Civil War, Guinness exemplified a rare constant—poured and shared even as mortar fire cracked

---

[13] Fiona Audley, "Former Pub Where Michael Collins Convened Intelligence Unit Meetings Gets Heritage Plaque," Irish Post, April 7, 2024, https://www.irishpost.com/history/former-pub-where-michael-collins-convened-intelligence-unit-meetings-gets-heritage-plaque-270603 (accessed August 22, 2025).

in the distance. In pubs across Ireland, it was one of the few things both sides still agreed on. Tensions simmered. Plans were whispered in snugs and corners. But the pint created a space where silence could settle. And sometimes, silence was a beginning.

In other places where the war stayed in the background, the ritual continued unchanged. Guinness flowed as it always had—steady, familiar, and unbroken.

Martin McDonagh's *The Banshees of Inisherin* captures this landscape of quiet devastation in allegory. A remote island, untouched by battles, echoes with distant cannon fire from the mainland. Two friends played by Brendan Gleeson and Colin Farrell—Colm and Pádraic—embark on their own bitter civil war. The pub is central, as always. Guinness is there, unspoken but ever present, anchoring the scenes where friendship frays, where nothing makes sense anymore except the next pint.

When Pádraic sees fighting on the mainland, he offers a whispered prayer of *"Good luck to you. Whatever it is you're fighting about"* and later when he is left outcast from the pub to sit on a wall with Dominic, the village misfit, he reflects and asks him if he had seen it. Dominic's answer— *"Me, I pay no attention to wars. I'm again' [against] 'em. Wars and soap."*—it isn't just comic relief. It's resignation.

By the end, both men have lost everything: the pony, the sister, the fingers, the house, the music, the innocence — and Dominic. And yet they're still there—together, somehow. On the same island. With nowhere else to go. No peace, but no escape. Just the wreckage between them and maybe, still, a pint to share in silence.

The Guinness brewery, still officially apolitical, had become something more than neutral. It was a steady marker in a country tearing itself apart, a placeholder for the idea that something—anything—might remain after the last explosion. In a nation desperate for symbols that would outlast the war, the pint stood tall. Still poured. Still shared. Still here.

CULTURAL GRAVITY IN A FRAGMENTED COUNTRY

As the guns quieted, Ireland began the painful work of defining itself. What did it mean to be Irish now? Who would write the new national story? Writers. Poets. Playwrights. Publicans. And Guinness.

It was served in Abbey Theatre bars, in working-class pubs, in student unions, and military messes. It had no side. But it had weight. And that made it matter.

By 1925, Ireland had changed forever. The British flag no longer flew above Dublin Castle. But St. James's Gate remained unchanged—its barrels rolling, its name intact, its glassware polished.

Over its first 150 years, Guinness had survived wars, both foreign and domestic, maintained its business, preserved the loyalty of both Ireland and Britain, and emerged as a true Irish cornerstone.

Its secret? It didn't sell revolution. It served continuity. And in doing so, it became part of the revolution, whether it meant to or not.

In the years that followed, a strange thing happened: Guinness became a symbol of the new Ireland. Not officially. Not anointed. But emotionally.

Guinness was local, but respected worldwide. Guinness was traditional, but modernizing fast. Guinness was Irish, but unapologetically successful. And subliminally. Guinness is as quintessentially Irish as Ireland itself appropriating the harp as its very symbol.

So intertwined are the symbols of Guinness and Ireland, that the harp itself, the only musical instrument to serve as an official national symbol, had to be registered by the Irish Free State government from the opposite side as that of the famous Guinness usage which was copyrighted in 1876.[14]

The pint had earned its place. Not through politics. Not through slogans. But through presence. Through staying. Through pouring when everything else was burning.

---

[14] The Irish Post, "Irish Harp: did Ireland's national symbol come from Guinness?," The Irish Post, accessed May 25, 2025, https://www.irishpost.com/life-style/irish-harp-did-irelands-national-symbol-come-from-guinness-235523

4 FROM NATIONAL SYMBOL TO GLOBAL EXPORT

"Wherever you go in the world, if there's Guinness on tap, you're never too far from home."
– Irish emigrant saying

Symbols don't just survive—they travel. After Ireland's fight for identity, Guinness crossed oceans as an unspoken ambassador, becoming proof that something Irish could endure, expand, and still feel entirely its own.

The smoke from the revolution had barely cleared when Ireland began the impossible: building a nation out of ashes. By the mid-1920s, the new Irish Free State was scarred, split, and uncertain. Infrastructure was broken. Trust was fragile. The economy was shaky.

That Guinness became a global brand is a remarkable story on its own. But when held against the backdrop of Ireland's colonial past, it becomes something closer to miraculous.

For over 400 years, the English systematically suppressed Ireland's ability to trade freely. From the late 15th century through the 18th, Irish industries—from wool to dairy, from glass to brewing—were constrained, taxed, or outright banned in order to favor English producers. Irish merchants were denied access to imperial markets, and any flourishing domestic industry was quickly clipped before it could spread.

The extent of this suppression is captured plainly in Seumas MacManus's *The Story of the Irish Race*. Writing in 1944, he summarized the consequences of these embargos with haunting clarity:

> *And thus is explained in part why Ireland, one of the most favoured by nature, and one of the most fertile countries in Europe is yet one of the poorest. And why it is that, as recent statistics show, ninety-eight per cent of the export trade of the three kingdoms is in the hands of Britain—and in Ireland's hands, two per cent.* [15]

And yet—out of that long arc of suppression, a single Irish stout rose up, crossed the sea, and built an empire of its own. Guinness didn't just survive the chokehold of English trade policy—it outgrew it. The very thing they tried to

---

[15] Seumas MacManus, *The Story of the Irish Race*, 4th rev. ed. (New York: The Devin-Adair Company, 1944), 492.

deny the Irish—a product the world would crave—was born in Dublin and poured across continents.

To drink a Guinness abroad is not just to taste Ireland. It is, in some quiet way, to witness a reversal of economic gravity. What was once held back, now flows forward. What was once suppressed, now saturates.

Guinness was steady.

While new governments debated and new flags were raised, the barrels at St. James's Gate kept rolling. Guinness had weathered empire. It had brewed through rebellion. And now, it was poised to become something more than a survivor.

It would become a symbol of who Ireland could be.

Even in song, Guinness traveled. In the famously exaggerated Irish folk ballad *The Irish Rover*, the ship's absurd cargo includes, among other things,

> *We had one million bags of the best Sligo rags*
> *We had two million barrels of bones*
> *We had three million bales of old nanny goats' tails*
> *We had four million barrels of stone*
> *We had five million dogs, six million hogs*
> *Seven million barrels of porter*
> *We had eight million hides of old blind horses' eyes*
> *In the hold of the Irish Rover*

It's a joke, sure. But it's also a kind of truth. In the Irish imagination, Guinness was essential cargo—on any journey, real or mythical.

EXPORTING MORE THAN A DRINK

By the late 1920s, Guinness had become Ireland's single most valuable export. It wasn't just beer—it was brand. It carried weight. It carried story.

As Irish emigrants left in waves—searching for work in London, Liverpool, Boston, New York—they took two things with them: songs, and Guinness. The pint became a portable homeland, a sensory shortcut to the streets and voices they missed.

But something else was happening, people outside Ireland wanted it, too.

In cities and colonies still echoing with British influence, Guinness was a taste of both heritage and hierarchy. It became fashionable in London clubs, reliable in West African ports, and mystical in the Caribbean. Wherever it went, it carried with it the flavor of Ireland—but also the aura of permanence.

THE QUIET AMBASSADOR

Unlike other brands that shouted their way into markets, Guinness whispered. Edward Cecil Guinness was notorious for his disdain of advertising.

During the 1800's most pubs in England were brewery-owned ventures. Built in distribution for their product directly to the consumer, but Guinness never joined this practice focusing instead on production and transportation. Bottling was left up to local agents who often would represent Guinness under its own label, sometimes mentioning Guinness, or including the harp trademark, but more typically creating their own brand.

The power of the pint of Guinness was being felt, but it wasn't necessarily even known by its real name. It wasn't until Guinness began to centralize distribution and take control of its branding that the name itself started to carry the same weight as the liquid inside.

As Independence was achieved, and modern sensibility of the Irish tradition began to take root, Guinness changed its tune and marketing and advertising grew it's role in the company's success. Its message was never "Buy This Beer"—it was always, "This is the beer of people who know who they are."

In post-colonial Ireland, trying to forge a national identity out of broken narratives, this was gold.

Guinness became a kind of unofficial ambassador. It said to the world:

"We may be small, but we are resilient.
We may be poor, but we are proud.
And we may be quiet, but we endure."

Tourism boards couldn't have written it better.

THE PINT BECOMES THE FLAG

There's a reason you don't see many Irish flags hanging in Irish pubs around the world.

You see pints.

The Guinness logo—harp and all—became the de facto flag of the diaspora.

The harp was no arbitrary design choice. It was a stroke of genius by Benjamin Lee Guinness, third-generation head of the family business, inspired by the legend of Brian Boru. On Good Friday in 1014, Boru led a singular battle in Irish history—the Battle of the Weir of Clontarf—where 20,000 Irish faced an equal Viking force of Danes and Scots. The battle ended in victory for Boru, but also in his death, killed by a Danish spy in his encampment after the battle had been won. Viking power in Ireland was broken forever, yet with the loss of their High King, Ireland also lost its compass.[16] From his demise rose a legacy more enduring than his reign: a symbol of Irish identity that would, centuries later, be housed in the library of Trinity College Dublin.

Among Ireland's treasures is a medieval harp, long associated with Brian Boru. Though it almost certainly dates from the 15th century—crafted from oak and willow with twenty-nine brass strings—it remains the oldest of its kind in Ireland and became the model for the emblem of the Irish state. By Benjamin Lee's time, the harp was already deeply woven into the fabric of Irish identity.[17]

That connection was personal. The site of Boru's final battle was, some eight and a half centuries later, part of Benjamin

---

[16] MacManus, *The Story of the Irish Race*, 4th rev. ed, 280-283
[17] Trinity College Dublin, *The Long Room*, September 2015, accessed August 9, 2025, https://www.tcd.ie/library/old-library/long-room.

Lee's own St. Anne's estate.[18] He was uniquely positioned to recognize the power of the symbol and to make it central to Guinness's identity—not only because of this historical tie, but because, unlike his father and grandfather, he was the first Guinness to lead the brewery without also serving as head brewer. That role belonged has been handed to John Purser, Arthur II's junior partner, and then to his son John Tertius Purser.

Freed from the daily demands of brewing, Benjamin Lee could devote himself entirely to the business, to civic and political life, to philanthropy, and to shaping Guinness's public identity and legacy. His genius was to root the brand in a symbol bound to Ireland's oldest fight for independence, anchoring a beer in the very soil of Irish memory and pride.

It was in the lit signs, the coasters, the taps. To the second-generation Irish in New York, the homesick in Australia, and the curious in Tokyo, Guinness didn't just represent Ireland—it represented memory.

It became a way of saying, I belong to somewhere that still matters to me.

And for people who weren't Irish—but wanted to taste a story with depth—Guinness was a gentle invitation.

---

[18] Michele Guinness, *The Guinness Legend*, 81

REDEFINING IRISHNESS

In the mid-20th century, Ireland still carried the stereotypes of poverty, pain, and provincialism. Guinness offered a counter-narrative.

It was clean. Global. Sophisticated. Yet still distinctly Irish.

For a country fighting to move past its trauma without forgetting it, Guinness was perfect: it didn't erase the past— it brewed it into something enduring.

The Irish government leaned into this, often using Guinness as part of broader cultural export strategies. It was proof that Ireland didn't just mourn—it made. It didn't just suffer—it succeeded.

GUINNESS IN WORLD WAR II

When the Second World War broke out, Guinness faced a paradox. Ireland remained officially neutral, yet Guinness was essential to the morale of British troops. The stout was rationed at home, but kegs were still shipped to soldiers abroad.

In London, bombed-out pubs did their best to keep Guinness on tap. For many, a pint of the black stuff was a reminder of normalcy—of home, of continuity, of something that war could not entirely shatter. *"Guinness is good for you,"* the advertisements still said, even as Europe tore itself apart.

In 1942, when Ireland restricted barley malting and banned beer exports to protect bread supplies, the sudden Guinness shortage in Belfast stirred unrest among British troops.

Whitehall[19] moved quickly, arranging a barter: wheat in exchange for stout. Soon another snag appeared—Guinness warned it lacked coal to brew enough for both Ireland and export. The British, eager to keep soldiers supplied, released coal shipments across the Irish Sea.

This pattern repeated itself in the run-up to D-Day. Guinness became a bargaining chip: Britain offered wheat, coal, fertilizer, and machinery in return for the stout that kept Allied forces content. Those exchanges not only ensured the pint still flowed in Northern Ireland but also provided neutral Ireland with resources that sustained its delicate balance through the war.[20]

Back in Dublin, pints remained scarcer, the supply carefully guarded. People grumbled, but they understood. Guinness had become not just Ireland's drink, but the drink of the wider world. Even in a time of rations and ruin, the company ensured that the stout still flowed where it mattered most.

---

[19] **"Whitehall"** refers to the central offices of the British government and senior civil service, named after the street in Westminster, London, where many of the key ministries are located.
[20] Bryce Evans, "How Guinness Saved Ireland," Irish America, June 2014, https://www.irishamerica.com/2014/05/how-guinness-saved-ireland/ (accessed August 22, 2025).

THE GLOBAL FACE OF LOCAL PRIDE

By the 1950s and '60s, Guinness was not just an Irish brand—it was an international institution. Breweries in Cameroon. Production in Malaysia. Exports everywhere.

Today, the largest consumer of Guinness is the UK (Ireland comes in second). Nigeria is third, and then the US and Cameroon; and finally, Kenya, Ghana, Indonesia, Malaysia, and Canada round out the top ten.

Guinness has become so successful abroad that in some countries they consider it their national beer. Workers who produce Foreign Extra Stout in Nigeria's brewery don't quite comprehend why Guinness is even sold in Ireland.

Yet, when they find themselves there and enjoy themselves a bottle just like one that they would have back home, it is then that their experience of the familiar will resonate with the essence of being genuinely Guinness.

For much of the world, the Guinness they know isn't what's poured in Irish pubs—it's Foreign Extra Stout. First brewed in the early 1800s, it was designed to travel. Stronger, darker, and more bitter than Guinness Draught, it was fortified to withstand long sea journeys to the Caribbean, Africa, and Southeast Asia.

But it didn't just arrive. It stayed. In Nigeria and Jamaica, Guinness Foreign Extra Stout is a beloved national pint. In Malaysia and Ghana, it's tied to strength and heritage. It's often bottled, often shared, and often brewed locally under license. It's Guinness—but refracted through a different lens. A little louder. A little bolder. Still part of the family.

It reminds us that Irishness isn't always quiet—and Guinness isn't always what you expect.

Some feared expansion at this scale would lead to dilution. But back home in Dublin, the gates of St. James's remain at the center of its reach. And that matters.

You can tour the place now. Pour your own pint. Get a certificate. It sounds like a gimmick—until you do it. Then it feels like a kind of reverence. You're not just pouring a beer. You're stepping into a ritual people have practiced, perfected, and passed on for generations.

Because while Guinness had gone global, it had never gone generic. It kept its rituals. Its quiet. Its sense of occasion.

It is not a beer for parties. It is a beer for pauses. And that has made universal. And made it eternal.

THE POUR THAT MADE IT POSSIBLE

To understand how Guinness became a global brand, you have to understand how the pint itself changed.

For centuries, Guinness was drawn straight from wooden casks, poured by gravity taps or pulled through hand-pumps. There was no standard. No ceremony. Just stout—sometimes flat, sometimes frothy, always a little unpredictable. The pint you got depended on the barkeep, the barrel, and the moment.

Bottled Guinness, when it became widely available, brought something new: control. And with it, perhaps, the beginning of ritual. A bottle was uncapped. A partial pour into a single glass. The rest left to the drinker, who topped it off to taste.

The next round? A new bottle—but the same glass, reused like a familiar friend. Quietly, a kind of participation was born. A shared act between barkeep and drinker. The pint began to matter not just for how it tasted, but *how it was given and received.*

Then, in 1959—on the brewery's 200th anniversary— Guinness changed everything again. It introduced nitrogenation: a blend of nitrogen (N_2) and carbon dioxide (CO_2) that transformed the experience. The mouthfeel turned creamy and smooth. The famous cascade began— those mesmerizing swirling bubbles that settle into stillness. And finally, the head: dense, tight, almost sculptural, sitting atop the glass like it had always been there.

Pioneered by Guinness Master Brewer Michael Ash, the problem they set out to solve was the use of modern keg systems and the unfortunate reality that by its very character did not pour well from systems using CO_2 alone. The result was then a pint that could be poured from the keg, but it also turned the pint into a performance.

This innovation allowed Guinness to standardize the experience, even as it expanded. Whether you were in Dublin or Dubai, the pint could feel familiar.

Some traditionalists bristled at the change. They missed the cask character, the raw charm of the old ways. But most embraced it. Because nitrogenation didn't erase Guinness's soul—it amplified it.

This wasn't just chemistry. It was choreography. The Guinness pour became a performance—and for the first time, it asked for *patience*.

Guinness didn't just export barrels.
It exported a ritual.

HOW THE WORLD TASTED IRELAND

Here's what's remarkable:

When most people around the world tasted Guinness for the first time, they weren't just tasting a stout—they were tasting Ireland.

And unlike other cultural exports, Guinness didn't lean on cliché. No leprechauns. No plastic shamrocks. It let the liquid speak for itself. Dark, but not bitter. Strong, but not aggressive. Balanced. Intentional. Worth the wait. It became a liquid metaphor for the Irish spirit.

THE PINT AS PROOF

In a world where nations try endlessly to define their "brand," Ireland had an ace in the glass. It didn't need a slogan. It had a pour.

Every pint served in Paris or Pretoria was proof that Ireland wasn't just a country that endured tragedy—it was a country that made beauty. In flavor. In form. In legacy.

Guinness, exported, became not just economic power, but cultural proof.

It didn't ask for attention. It earned reverence. And in doing so, it lifted the image of Ireland everywhere it went.

5 GUINNESS IN THE MODERN IRISH IMAGINATION

"It is not what we say about our beer that matters, it is what our beer says about us."
– Guinness advertising archive

Even as Guinness moved through ports and customs, its real power lay in what it stirred at home. In modern Ireland, the pint became not only iconic, but reflective—shaped by the people who drank it, remembered it, and made it mean more.

The pint is no longer just a drink. It's a destination.

You don't just visit the Guinness Storehouse.

You ascend it.

In the heart of Dublin, where Guinness was born, the Storehouse isn't just a brewery tour—it's a cathedral of brand, story, and ritual. With over 20 million visitors since opening in 2000, it is now Ireland's most visited tourist attraction.

But it's not just tourists. It's the diaspora. The dreamers. The descendants. The curious. The proud. They come not to taste something new, but to touch something old—something that lives between culture and memory.

Walking those floors—past barley, yeast, water, and time—you realize Guinness has stopped being just a product.

It's become a myth we can walk through.

BRANDING THAT TOLD A STORY— WITHOUT TELLING YOU TO BUY

Guinness has always understood something most brands still struggle to learn: people don't remember ads—they remember how ads make them feel. From the start, Guinness didn't sell a buzz. It sold a belief.

In the 1930s, they said, *"Guinness is Good for You"*—not as a scientific claim, but as a quiet suggestion, a wink that understood the emotional comfort of the pint. Then came the surrealism: sea lions balancing glasses, toucans in flight, harps, slogans laced with gentle wit. These weren't campaigns; they were characters in a story you wanted to join.

By the time the modern era arrived, Guinness was ready with *Surfer*—a thunderous black-and-white epic of anticipation and reward. Then *Made of More*. Then the slow-motion pour and its now-iconic whisper: *"Good things come to those who wait."* No neon. No noise. Just patience, power, and presence.

It's a masterclass in advertising—emotional selling decades ahead of its time. Because each ad wasn't about beer. It was

47

about temperament. Guinness wasn't fast—it was deliberate. It wasn't loud—it was meaningful. It wasn't for everyone—and that was exactly the point.

It's not a party drink.
It's a story drink.
And in Ireland, storytelling is sacred.

THE PINT AS MEMORY MACHINE

Ask an Irish person abroad what they miss most, and they might say family, sea air, or the sound of rain.

But right after that?

A proper pint.

There's a joke in Dublin: Guinness doesn't travel. But it's not about shipping. It's about soul. Drinking Guinness in Ireland isn't just about taste—it's about context.

The temperature of the glass.
The sound of the settle.
The feel of the pub around you.

Guinness has mastered something few brands ever achieve: it's not just selling product—it's selling nostalgia in real time.

THE PINT AS PASSPORT

For Irish people abroad, Guinness becomes a kind of cultural credential.

Order one in a foreign pub, and the bartender might smile knowingly. Pull out your Irish passport and follow it with a pint—and suddenly you're not a tourist. You're home, briefly.

The pint itself can be just as powerful a passport establish one's Irish identity. Barack Obama, 44th President of the United States used it in just such a manner, proclaiming, *"My name is Barack Obama, of the Moneygail Obamas and I've come home to find the apostrophe we lost somewhere along the way"* all the while drinking a pint of Guinness.[21]

Even for those without Irish blood, the pint is a bridge. It's a way to honor something real. To say, I may not be from Ireland, but I understand something about what it values.

In that way, Guinness is one of the few global brands that feels like a permission slip to belong.

Sometimes you walk into a bar expecting a drink and find a piece of your past—or a hint of someone else's. You don't need heritage to recognize something as real. You feel it in the glass. You feel it in how the staff talk about the pour, the lineage, the quiet pride that fills a room when they get it right.

A STEWARD OF IRISH MEMORY

In the Guinness podcast *Behind the Guinness Gates* hosted by Irish historian Turtle Bunbury, brewer and Flavor Essence

---

[21]Turtle Bunbury, *The Irish Diaspora: Tales of Emigration, Exile and Imperialism* (New York: Thames & Hudson, Ltd., 2021), 243.

Manager, Kate Curran shared a quiet story that echoed loudly. She's a fifth-generation Guinness employee—though she only knew of three. A few years ago, her father and uncle visited the Guinness Archives together and discovered two more generations going back to 1865. What struck her was the surprise—but also the *stewardship*. That Guinness, as a company, had kept the records. That it cares enough to remember what her family had forgotten.[22]

In an era when genealogy has become digital and personal—an act of searching for lost threads—Guinness stands as an institution that not only invites that search, but *safeguards* it. It becomes a mirror for Irish identity itself: fractured, resilient, and slowly pieced together across generations.

This emotional resonance doesn't stop at the bar. You see it ripple into music and film too. Guinness doesn't just appear—it haunts. It echoes in the background of The Dubliners' ballads, the punk grit of The Pogues, or the clenched-fist pride of Dropkick Murphys. It's a chorus and a confessional. The glass doesn't just hold a drink—it holds tone. And Irish storytelling, in every medium, honors that.

One of the most telling moments comes in *The Commitments*, that raw, kinetic portrait of working-class

---

[22] Kate Curran, interview by Turtle Bunbury, *"Sense of Flavour,"* *Behind the Guinness Gates*, audio podcast, March 28, 2023, https://open.spotify.com/episode/73elK5vba1tvob9nlqAFe1.

Dublin. Amid the chaos of the club, Deco—the soulful voice of the band strides up to the bar and emphatically orders *"a glass of the black."* No product placement. No branded tap. Just the language of belonging. No Irish person needed to ask what he meant. It wasn't a Guinness™—it was *the* Guinness. A nod to how deeply the pint is embedded in identity. In Ireland, the pint names itself.

Not just a product. Not just a company.
A keeper of names. A recorder of belonging.

HARP LAGER AND THE MODERN SHIFT

As Ireland entered the 1960s, Guinness found itself at a crossroads. The stout still symbolized tradition, but a new generation of drinkers—at home and abroad—began craving something lighter, something different. The black pint still ruled the tap, but whispers of lager and continental influence were growing louder.

That's when Guinness brewed up something entirely new.

In 1960, Guinness made a bold move: it entered the lager market. The traditional stout had long defined its brand, but as continental lagers like Heineken and Carlsberg gained popularity among younger drinkers and international markets, Guinness responded by launching a new brew— Harp Lager.

Brewed at the newly developed Great Northern Brewery in Dundalk, Harp represented more than just diversification. It was a strategic attempt to remain relevant and competitive in a changing world. To ensure quality and authenticity,

Guinness brought in Dr. Herman Muender, a German brewing expert, to lead the development.

By 1961, Harp's promise had grown strong enough that Guinness joined forces with other major brewers—Courage, Scottish & Newcastle, Bass, and Mitchells & Butlers—to form Harp Lager Ltd., a cooperative effort to market and distribute the beer widely.

Harp's branding retained a strong connection to Ireland. It adopted the same Brian Boru harp, the national symbol, and the emblem that is Guinness, as its logo—asserting Irish heritage even as it introduced a distinctly continental taste. In a way, this was Guinness signaling that modernity didn't require abandoning identity.

The Dundalk facility continued brewing Harp until 2013, when production moved to Guinness's iconic St. James's Gate Brewery in Dublin. Today, Harp Lager is still poured across pubs in Ireland and Northern Ireland, often as the counterpoint to Guinness Stout on the same tap bank.

It wasn't as culturally seismic as the black pint, but Harp represented Guinness's evolving relationship with its market. It showed that Guinness could both honor tradition and innovate without compromise. In its own way, Harp is proof that Irish brewing could speak more than one language—and still be understood as deeply Irish.

GUINNESS AND THE STORYTELLERS

Writers drink it. Artists reference it. Musicians toast with it. Not because they're told to—but because it belongs. Guinness doesn't chase attention. It lingers in the background, steady as a rhythm. You won't always notice it, but when you do, it feels like it was always meant to be there.

That presence wasn't built by ad campaigns or corporate slogans—not at first. In its earliest decades of growth, Guinness didn't advertise at all. It didn't need to. The company relied on its bottlers and merchants to spread the brand. These independent agents distributed the beer, often under their own labels, and handled the sales pitch themselves. For a time, Guinness was one of the most consumed drinks in Ireland—without most people even realizing they were drinking Guinness. The liquid had a reputation long before the brand caught up.

Edward Cecil Guinness preferred it that way. He believed advertising was a wasteful indulgence—beneath the stature of a product that should speak for itself. He wasn't wrong. For a while, the pint did all the work. But as the 20th century marched forward and competitors became louder, more visual, and more emotionally clever, the pressure to evolve became unavoidable.

Rupert Guinness) saw it coming. Unlike his father, he understood that the modern consumer wasn't just drinking a stout—they were adopting a symbol. And if Guinness was going to enter the world of advertising, it wouldn't be to follow trends. It would be to outclass them. The brewery hired S.H. Benson as its first official advertising agency in 1927 and launched a campaign rooted not in aspiration, but observation. A survey of drinkers in Dublin pubs asked a simple question: Why do you drink Guinness? The most common answer became the headline of the first campaign:

"Guinness is good for you."

Even James Joyce tried to get in on it. He once mailed the brewery a suggested line of his own—*"The free, the flow, the frothy freshener."*[23] It didn't make the cut. Guinness had already found a more grounded poetry, drawn not from the literary elite but from the lived experiences of its drinkers.

That's why Guinness shows up quietly in the corners of songs and poems, the soft light of pub scenes, the still glass beside a battered notebook. It doesn't interrupt the story. It deepens it.

There's a certain kind of creative moment where a pint is more than a drink—it's punctuation. A pause. A permission to feel something. And whether it's raised at a reading in Boston, a concert in Berlin, or a wedding in Melbourne, when someone lifts a Guinness, they're not just joining the toast. They're entering the story.

No tagline required. Just the weight of the glass, the hush that follows a pour, and the knowing glance that says: **this** means something.

And then there's *The Workman's Friend*—a sly, knowing poem by Flann O'Brien, better known by its iconic closing line: *"A pint of plain is your only man."*

---

[23] Rory Guinness. *World of Guinness*. London: Scala Arts & Heritage Publishers Ltd., 2025, p. 82.

In the 2005 cultural homage *Dublin Presented by Ronnie Drew*[24], Together, with other members of The Dubliners, they take turns reciting each stanza, passing the poem like a shared pint. No branding. No tap handles. Just lived experience. Ronnie opens the piece with that unmistakable voice—half gravel, half gospel—and after each man offers his verse, it's Ronnie who closes it, anchoring the moment with a final, familiar nod.

Not once is Guinness named. But it's the only thing being spoken about. The *"pint of plain"* isn't a stand-in—it's a stand-in that has outlived the original name.

As Flann O'Brien wrote:

> *When things go wrong and will not come right,*
> *Though you do the best you can,*
> *When life looks black as the hour of night—*
> *A pint of plain is your only man.*[25]

That's not branding. That's belief.

GUINNESS IN THE NEW IRELAND

Today's Ireland is not the Ireland of the 1916 rebels. It's younger. More diverse. More global. More wired to the

---

[24] *Dublin Presented by Ronnie Drew*, DVD, directed by Peter Galligan (Dublin: Celtic Note Productions, 2005). Features members of The Dubliners reciting "The Workman's Friend" by Flann O'Brien.
[25] Flann O'Brien, *The Workman's Friend*, originally published in *At Swim-Two-Birds* (London: Longmans, Green and Co., 1939).

world. There are new voices, new flags, new questions. And yet... the pint remains.

Guinness has kept pace. It sponsors men's and women's rugby. It shows up at Pride. It backs mental health campaigns and pours just as easily for the old regulars as for the newly arrived. It holds the weight of history in one hand and reaches forward with the other. It has managed to be timeless without becoming tone-deaf.

In a country still working to balance its past and future, Guinness remains one of the few things that feels like it belongs to everyone.

And here's the thing—it's not just a feeling. Walk into any pub and look around: roughly one in every three pints being poured is a Guinness. Stout still makes up over a third of all beer consumed in Ireland. And nearly nine out of ten of those stouts? They're Guinness.[26]

---

[26] Based on 2023 and 2024 reporting: beer accounted for 42.9% of alcohol consumption in Ireland; stout represented 35.6% of beer; and Guinness commanded roughly 88% of the stout market, comprising 13.4% of Ireland's total pure alcohol intake. Sources include:

- MarketScreener, "Diageo: Ireland The Home of Guinness," 2025
- Anthony Foley, *Estimate of Alcohol Consumption per Adult in 2023* (Drinks Industry Group of Ireland, 2024)
- *Irish Beer Market Report*, Drinks Ireland IBEC, 2023
- *Scottish License Trade News*, "Stout Wars," 2023

It's not just that beer is the most consumed form of alcohol in the country. It's that Guinness is, by far, the stout of choice—still.

In a nation of shifting identities, that kind of staying power says something. It says that what Guinness stands for—ritual, presence, connection—still speaks to the soul of the place.

And maybe that's the most Irish thing of all: to carry forward something old, quietly, and deliberately, and keep finding new meaning in it. Pint by pint.

NEVER WALK ALONE ON MATCH DAY

There's an old joke: *"What are the two major religions in Ireland today?"* The answer? *"Manchester United and Liverpool."*

Irish pubs around the globe tune in every weekend, filled with local supporters of one or the other. At Boland's it's Liverpool.

Some mornings, the place belongs entirely to the Reds. It doesn't matter if kickoff is at 7:00 am, 11:00 am, or 3:00 pm — the doors open, and the regulars file in. What started as a handful of faithful has grown into a group well over a hundred strong. At the 2025 Premier League trophy lift, more than 140 of us were here, from 8 months to 80 years old, singing together.

It's not just match days. Boland's has a night for live music, comedy, and trivia, and the next day, the pub turns into Anfield-by-way-of-Massachusetts. A few of us are lucky enough to cross over — singing along to a band one night, belting *You'll Never Walk Alone* the next morning.

This is one of a million community supporters' groups that form at local pubs, each one a small world of its own. Guinness isn't the only thing poured here, but it's been a steady sponsor of the games that matter — rugby, soccer, the GAA — the sports that tie communities together.

At the center of it all is Ged. From Liverpool himself, he's the de facto head of the crew. A driver by trade, he often drinks Guinness 0.0, but his presence is anything but sober. He drove us all to our first Coronas concert and later led a pilgrimage of sorts to Liverpool with Barefoot Scott and Kevin in tow to watch the boys play at Anfield. A ticket, scarf, and program from that trip now hang proudly on the wall at Boland's — a framed reminder that this is more than a pub, more than a team.

It's a place where the match is only part of the story, and the people are the rest.

THE LEGACY BEYOND THE LABEL

The core of Guinness has stayed the same—but it hasn't stood still. In recent years, the brand has embraced experimentation through its Open Gate Brewery in Dublin, releasing limited runs of everything from Nitro Cold Brew Coffee Stout to Citra IPAs. These aren't trying to replace the classic pour. They're extensions—reminders that Guinness is both tradition and curiosity.

Some of them disappear after a season. Others—like the West Indies Porter or Antwerpen Stout—find lasting fans.

But each one reflects a kind of creative restlessness that doesn't undermine the original. It underscores it.

Because a brand that survives centuries doesn't do it by accident. It does it by knowing what never changes—and knowing how to change everything else.

THE PINT THAT BECAME THE MIRROR

What do we see when we look at a pint of Guinness today?

Not just a drink. Not just a brand.

We see memory. We see ritual. We see ourselves—quietly, clearly, without needing to explain why. It holds the weight of the past and the shape of the present. It reminds us who we were—and hints at who we still hope to be.

We see resilience in its darkness.
Patience in the way it settles.
Groundedness in its silence.
A rootedness that doesn't demand attention, but earns it.
And a strange, comforting truth: that something can be both old and new at once, if we let it.

Guinness doesn't change fast. And in a world that moves faster every day, that's exactly why it matters. It's not chasing the moment. It's holding space for it. It doesn't shout to be seen. It invites us to stop and notice.

In the glass, we don't just see a pint—we see a pause. A ritual. A reason to remember.

It is, quite simply, the drink that reflects us back to ourselves.

And remarkably, that reflection travels. Because even far from home, even in places where the accent has faded and the landscape is unfamiliar, the ritual remains.

You may not be in Ireland anymore.
But if the Guinness is good—you just might feel like you are.

After all, they've said from the start they plan to be around for 9,000 years. There's no rush.

6 A PINT ABROAD

"I can still taste Ireland in a pint, even after forty years away."
– Irish-American grandfather

What begins as a ritual in Ireland becomes something else entirely when carried across an ocean. For generations of the Irish abroad, Guinness has not only preserved identity—it has revealed it, one pint at a time.

You can't take Ireland with you—but you can pour it.

THE SHIP LEAVES, BUT THE PINT STAYS

From the 1840s through the 1950s, millions of Irish left their homeland—fleeing famine, poverty, or political hardship. Some left in silence. Others with songs. All of them left with a wound.

They couldn't bring the land.
They couldn't bring the family.
But one thing made its way across: Guinness.

Sometimes it followed years later. Sometimes it was already waiting in a dockside pub. And sometimes, it showed up in the stories whispered over teacups that slowly became pint glasses.

But when it appeared—whether in Brooklyn or Boston, Sydney, or South Africa—it wasn't just a drink.

It was the closest thing to home.

PUBS AS PORTALS

Irish pubs abroad have always been more than watering holes.

They are temples of memory.

Walk into one—anywhere in the world—and you'll find more than just signage or barstools.

You'll see surnames in gold leaf, Gaelic football flickering on a silent screen, and a child's photo behind the bar in a Communion suit. And always—a pint of Guinness poured with reverence.

For generations, these pubs have been the first landing place for Irish immigrants.

They offered more than drink. They offered job boards, housing tips, a familiar accent, a quiet nod.

A little dignity.

And a drink that reminded them of who they were—before the paperwork, before the distance.

As Barry put it during one of our conversations:

> *For me as an Irish person both at home and abroad, there is a sense of pride and identity in seeing the Guinness symbol or a pint of Guinness.*

Guinness isn't just served—it's stewarded. It helps carry the weight of Ireland and Irish identity, wherever it's poured.

Shuggy once shared the importance of the pint to him:

> *My mates back in Dublin, they post pictures of the pints they're having—and I post mine right back. I'm proud of my pour. I want them to see what it looks like here. What we've built here.*

For a pub to be Irish, truly Irish, it doesn't need shamrocks or shillelaghs on the wall. No leprechauns with clever sayings in the bathroom stalls. It needs something far less tangible—but instantly recognizable.

When you arrive at one of those true places, you know it.

It gets it.

It creates what Shuggy likes to call, a *"bubble"*—a feeling— that invites you to join it.

To make it your own.
To give it back what it gives you.
To make peace and find peace, all around a pint.

That's what a true Irish pub is all about.

But let's be clear—Irish pub culture isn't built on Guinness alone.

The pub is older than the pint.

People have gathered in these spaces for generations, with or without a drink in hand. Cider, wine, whiskey, even tea—

each has its place. What matters is the gathering. The listening. The quiet nods between strangers.

Guinness didn't invent pub culture. It doesn't own it, but it has become its most common companion—its most reliable passenger.

And more than any other drink—even Jameson, which arguably comes close—Guinness has carried the weight of that culture abroad. It didn't build the pub. But it's often the thing that helps the pub feel familiar, wherever you are.

Shuggy put it best when our daughter was preparing to spend a year abroad. With the certainty of someone who's lived it on both sides of the bar, he told her:

> *If you are ever away from home and find yourself in trouble, find the local Irish pub. You will be safe and they will help you. 100%.*

To him, the Guinness sign isn't just branding. It's a promise. A beacon. A way home.

It is, in many ways, the wings upon which the Irish pub took flight.

THE PINT AS CONNECTION POINT

In the diaspora, Guinness became more than nostalgia.

It became ritual—a drink on your father's anniversary, though he's buried in Clare. A birthday pint with a friend who shares your last name, even if your families haven't spoken in generations. A toast at an Irish wedding—in Texas.

And for second-generation Irish, Guinness offered something even more powerful: a thread back to something they didn't fully know but could feel.

To drink Guinness in the Bronx wasn't just to mimic Ireland—it was to reach for it.

And the opposite can be true as well. When someone you love decides to stay in Ireland, it does something to your sense of distance. The country becomes more than a place you visited. It becomes part of your story. And when you hold a Guinness in your hand, it doesn't feel like a souvenir—it feels like a thread.

A CANAL, A CORNER, AND A HOME TO THE PINT

Worcester, Massachusetts is a city that rarely makes the headlines but has always been at the crossroads. It also happens to be the home of my local—Boland's Bar and Patio.

Set midway between Boston and Providence, Worcester rose in the 19th century as a manufacturing hub tied first to the Blackstone Canal and then the Boston & Worcester Railroad. Irish laborers—first canal diggers, then railroad crews—laid down more than stone and track. They laid down a community. By the late 1800s, Worcester had one of the largest Irish Catholic populations in New England.

Today, Worcester still carries that legacy. The city remains a stronghold of Irish culture, proud of its parades, pubs, and diaspora threads that run across generations. It is here, in this unlikely but enduring Irish corner of New England, that the Guinness story takes root in ways both historic and personal. But the Irish pride Worcester shows every year on the Sunday before St. Patrick's Day stands in stark contrast to what the Irish first faced when they arrived.

Worcester's Irish identity began with a man named Tobias Boland, a contractor from Tipperary who, in 1826, brought hundreds of Irish laborers to dig the canal. At the time, his obituary recalled, there were only eighteen Catholic families in Worcester. Before Boland, Catholics could not even be buried in the city; their bodies had to be transported to Providence. He changed that, buying land in Worcester so his people could rest on their own ground.

The workers Boland employed built an encampment that grew into a shanty town on what became known as Green Island. When the winter frost stopped canal digging, Boland turned to building houses. When the canal was completed in 1828, he went on to build much more: the first building at The College of the Holy Cross in 1843, the first Catholic church in Worcester (St. John's) in 1845, and eventually helped to build the Cathedral of the Holy Cross in Boston which opened in 1875 though he did not live to see its completion..

By his death in 1883, Worcester's Catholic population had grown to thirty thousand. Boland and his crews had done more than dig—they built the infrastructure that opened Worcester to the world. The canal flowed south to Providence and the sea, and the railroad east to Boston's port. Those lines became lifelines: first for freight and coal, and soon enough for barrels of beer.[27]

By then, Guinness was already on the move. The brewery's first documented export to America came in 1817, with casks of stout landing in South Carolina. By the 1840s, Guinness was regularly shipped to New York. And in the 1870s, the Dublin firm E. & J. Burke became the exclusive export bottlers for the United States, ensuring that "Guinness's Extra Stout" could be found wherever Irish communities gathered.[28] With its canal, rail links, and rapidly growing Irish Catholic population, Worcester was exactly the kind of city where that demand would have been met.

It is easy to see why Shuggy named his bar "Boland's." The name is not just homage—it is inheritance. Worcester's Irish thirst for Guinness was made possible by the labor of Boland's canal crews, the very men who stayed to become the city's Irish community. Shuggy pours pints in that shadow, carrying the responsibility to make his pub the

---

[27] Margaret Boland and Thomas L. Rooney, *The Irish Pioneer: A Historical Novel of the Life of Tobias F. Boland* (Mobile, AL: Magnolia Mansions Press, 2009), 152–54, citing "Obituary of Tobias Francis Boland," *The Boston Pilot*, September 3, 1883.
[28] Aaron Goldfarb, "'We Don't Sell Stout. We Sell Guinness.' How One Irish Beer Became a Global Powerhouse," Wine Enthusiast, May 23, 2023, https://www.wineenthusiast.com/culture/beer/guinness-beer-history (accessed August 24, 2025).

same kind of gathering place where stories, songs, and identities take root.

That inheritance still sings in Worcester. Local musician Mike Ladd wrote a ballad called *Blackstone Cúil*[29], a tribute to the neighborhood where the canal once ran, where the Irish once scraped survival in a city that did not welcome them. The song tells of place and memory, of Worcester's Irish past and present, and names Tobias Boland directly:

> *Finally set foot in Americay,*
> *One of Mr. Boland's "Strollers,"*
> *digging canals in Yankeeland...*

From there, the ballad recounts the hostility the Irish faced in Worcester—mocked as "papist fools," warned away from places where they tried to settle, even marked by an invisible line of exclusion:

> *The Yankees all have eyes of blue lightening,*
> *And they sneer at us and call us papist fools*
> *And when that Blackstone river canal meets Lake*
>   *Quinsigamond,*
> *They draw a line where no Irish are to cross...*

Yet the song does not end in bitterness. It turns toward persistence: the labor that built railroads as well as canals,

---

[29] Mike Ladd, *Blackstone Cúil*, released June 1, 2015, track on *Blackstone Cúil*, Bandcamp, https://blackstonecuil.bandcamp.com/track/blackstone-c-il

the families raised on the margins, and the claim to a new kind of home in Worcester:

> *We settle where we can and raise our families,*
> *Our shovels help the railroad rise to rule*
> *And I will find my way, homesick but not astray,*
> *a new life in our place called Blackstone Cúil...*

And finally, the refrain that captures the transformation from encampment to permanence:

> *We dug our shovels in for the railroad run,*
> *and our tents grew into homes in Blackstone Cúil.*

The ballad captures the full arc: the immigrant leaving Ireland, laboring under Boland, facing Yankee scorn, and slowly turning tents into homes. In song, Worcester's Irish inheritance is remembered as both hardship and triumph— a corner of New England remade by Irish hands.

The word *cúil* (Irish for "corner") makes the song's title doubly resonant. *Blackstone Cúil* is not just a geographic marker; it is a cultural corner, a carved-out space where Worcester's Irish story continues to echo.[30]

---

[30] "***Cúil***" (pronounced roughly "cool") is an Irish word meaning "nook," "corner," or "secluded place." Its use in the song title suggests both the physical bend of the Blackstone and the cultural corner that Irish labor and life carved into Worcester.

POURING THE MYTH IN AMERICA

In cities like New York, Guinness became more than a drink. It was a signal—of belonging, of pride, of home. In some neighborhoods, the bar that poured the best pint was as well-known as the local church. These places became social altars where Irish Americans gathered not just to drink, but to *remember*—who they were, where they came from, and what it took to get there.

This reverence for ritual extended well beyond the bar. In the early 1900s, one of the clearest expressions of Irish identity and pride unfolded on the athletic fields of Queens. A group of Irish immigrants had formed the Irish American Athletic Club, welcoming all backgrounds, but rooted deeply in Irish working-class tenacity.

As historian Davy Holden explains in his Irish American History workshop,

> *The first African American, the first Jewish American, and the first Irish American to ever win an Olympic gold medal for the United States were all part of the Irish American Athletic Club, which is one of the most unbelievable stories I've ever heard.*[31]

Among its most iconic figures was Martin Sheridan, born in County Mayo in 1881. After emigrating to the U.S., he joined the New York Police Department, where he rose through

---

[31] Davy Holden, "Irish American History Workshop," Workshop (hosted online), July 10, 2025.

the ranks while excelling as an international athlete. As the Winged Fist archives recount, *"In 1906, after having served for several years with the NYPD, Sheridan was transferred to the Police Department's Main Office on Mulberry Street and made secretary of the Police Department Athletic Association."* [32] This gave him time and space to train while serving the public. He went on to win five Olympic gold medals and become a national figure.

"In addition to his Olympic and National Championships," the archive notes, *"Sheridan's athletic résumé includes the 1905 World All-Around Championship and eight national championships in discus throwing."* He also served in the NYPD's elite *"Italian Squad"* and later became *"chief of the Fifth Precinct Detectives."*

As Holden reflects, the Irish *"completely took over the police force—that was always a very common thing for Irish people to do for some reason is to join the police force."*

In men like Sheridan, Irish America found icons—figures who balanced toughness with principle, visibility with community pride. They didn't just assimilate—they competed, they led, and they won. And somewhere nearby, at the edge of a precinct or behind a corner bar, a pint of

---

[32] Ian McGowan, "Martin J. Sheridan: 'A Peerless Athlete,'" WingedFist.org, accessed July 14, 2025, http://www.wingedfist.org/Sheridan_peerless_athlete.html.

Guinness likely waited. It may not have been poured by today's standards—but it carried the same weight.

Only much later would Guinness codify the slow pour: the tulip glass, the temperature, the settle, the 119.5-second ritual. But in its slowness, Irish Americans recognized something familiar. The pour became a pause—a moment long enough to remember the people who came before you, who endured and built and rose. With every head settled and every pint served, it wasn't just a drink. It was a way to look back and say: they didn't guide us by shouting. They guided us by showing the way.

WELCOME HOME

In Irish homes, it's not always the tap that matters—it's the bottle in the fridge. Guinness Extra Stout, the bottled version with a slightly more bitter profile than Draught, is a staple on kitchen counters and family tables. It's often pulled out for gatherings, holidays, or those moments when a poured pint would be too much but a gesture is still needed.

It doesn't come with a surge or a ceremonial wait. But it holds something else: familiarity. It's the Guinness of uncles, of grandparents, of quiet after-dinner conversations. It's poured into mismatched glassware, passed across chipped tables, and sipped during reruns of the news.

It may not look like the showpiece. But it's every bit as sacred.

Barry shared with me once how his father, who wasn't a big drinker would enjoy a bottle at home from time to time.

He would particularly enjoy a drink after doing the
garden or cutting grass and the hedges in our back
and front gardens he would joke, "First one today and
badly needed!"! Dad would feel that he had earned the
pint bottle of Guinness and was a form of a reward for
the hours spent doing a long stint of gardening!

GUINNESS IN THE KITCHEN

In immigrant homes, especially during holidays, Guinness moved from the bar into the kitchen:

In stews and breads
In gravies and marinades
Poured out on the counter in a chipped mug while music played

It even followed into fiction and film. In the movie *Brooklyn*, a Guinness poured at a church dance completes the room— it hums beneath the music, anchoring the scene in something real. Or in *Waking Ned Devine*, a pint lifted at a funeral becomes joy and tradition at once. In *In America*, it's grief and silence in a glass—what's left when words fail.

For families who didn't have much, the presence of Guinness on the table gave the meal weight. It made it Irish. It made it whole.

THE PINT THAT HELPS PEOPLE GRIEVE

Many Irish immigrants carried not just hope, but trauma. And grief needs ritual.

For some, Guinness became a mourning companion:

Poured quietly the night someone died.
Raised gently at the funeral meal.
Sipped while stories made the pain bearable.
Held high as *"The Parting Glass"* is played at family reunions

Because Guinness doesn't demand a party. It allows presence that makes it a companion of healing, not just celebration.

GUINNESS TODAY: A PINT WITH ECHO

Now, decades later, many descendants of the Irish diaspora don't know the language. They've never been to Dublin. But they know how to pour a pint. And they know how to sit with it.

That's the power of Guinness.

It's not a memory. It's a living echo. And that echo—raised in a bar in Boston, whispered over a glass in Chicago, captured in a blurry family photo—is what keeps Ireland near.

Even when it's far.

A PINT THAT OUTLIVED AN EMPIRE

Before Ireland won its independence, Guinness offered a glimpse of what independence could look like.

In a country where Irishness was often synonymous with poverty, subservience, and exile, Guinness stood apart. It was proudly Irish. It paid better. It built homes. It offered pensions, clinics, and clubhouses. It gave workers—many of them Dublin-born Catholics—a reason to believe they mattered. And perhaps most powerfully, it did all of this under the nose of Empire.

Guinness didn't speak in revolutionary slogans. But it didn't have to. Its impact was lived, not shouted. In an era where Irish voices were suppressed, where even the teaching of the Irish language was discouraged, Guinness offered another kind of identity: one that came with dignity on the pay slip and pride in the craft.

What's more remarkable is this: as Guinness became a global export, it carried that dignity with it—not the image of the crown.

By the mid-19th century, barrels of Guinness were traveling with British troops and merchants across the globe—to India, Africa, the Caribbean, Australia. Wherever the Union Jack landed, there too came the black pint. But while its transport was imperial, its essence was Irish. Subtly, stubbornly, it was not colonized by the Empire—it colonized back.

What other Irish export stood proudly on the shelves of Johannesburg, Lagos, Delhi, or Sydney—and was loved not because it was British, but precisely because it wasn't?

As post-colonial independence movements stirred in the 20th century, Guinness was often already there—familiar, local, part of the social ritual. In Nigeria, Guinness became so embedded that it eventually opened a brewery in 1962, just two years after Nigerian independence. In Jamaica, in Malaysia, in Singapore—the pint stayed, even when the British left.

And back home, the pint never lost its meaning. Even after Irish independence in 1922, Ireland struggled to stand tall. The country was still impoverished, rural, and beholden to larger powers. Many argue that it wasn't until Ireland joined the European Economic Community in 1973—or until the quiet revolution of its dairy cooperatives took hold—that its modern success truly began.

Some credit the butter industry with doing more than Guinness to lift the country out of Third World status. At The Butter Museum in Cork, you can trace that story in hand-churned timelines and export milestones, a reminder that rural collaboration and collective pride helped feed the world. Guinness may have symbolized Irish quality, but butter—and the farmers behind it—turned that symbolism into economic substance.

Still, Guinness had already laid the groundwork for something deeper—a psychological independence, a sense that Irish enterprise could succeed, could endure, and could lead.

It may not have hoisted a tricolor or sounded a marching drum, but the Guinness brand did something radical: it said to the world, *"This is Irish. And this is excellent."* No footnote. No apology.

That's how the pint helped unravel the empire—quietly, confidently, by modeling an identity that didn't ask for permission.

It showed colonized people, including the Irish, that you could be more than what Empire called you. You could be yourself. And still thrive.

And isn't that, in the end, the most revolutionary act of all?

THE ECHO CONTINUES

Even now, generations removed from famine or flight, the echo remains.

A young woman moves to Ireland and finds something in the rhythm of the place—its people, its work, its song. She builds a life there. She stays. And her family, miles away, begins to feel the pull too. They visit. They listen. They return changed.

Back home, they hear about a new Irish bar. A small place. Nothing flashy. But they go—maybe chasing a memory, maybe chasing a feeling.

And then the pint arrives. It settles. It's familiar and foreign all at once.
Not because of the taste.
Because of the weight of meaning in the glass.

This is how Guinness continues to work—not just in marketing or history books, but in quiet personal migrations of the heart.

Sometimes you don't choose Ireland.
It finds you.

And sometimes, all it takes is a pour to remind you that something important has already begun.

7 THE PINT THAT POURED THROUGH THE DIVIDE

The important Anglo-Irish reset is now under way.
– Simon Harris, Irish Taoiseach

In a nation where symbols once divided, one poured across both sides. During the Troubles, Guinness was more than a drink—it was a rare constant in a fractured land, offering quiet over chaos, and presence over provocation.

On one of our family trips to Ireland, we visited the North. We sat in a snug at the Crown Liquor Saloon in Belfast. It was lunchtime. Quiet. We ate and had a few pints. It was the only place I'd been to in the whole of the island where the bartender finished the pour with a shamrock drawn into the foam—a small flourish, done by an Englishman, funny enough, who seemed to understand the moment better than we expected.

The Crown has stood through more than most. It was bombed at least four times during the Troubles—not because of what it believed, but because of what it represented. A landmark. A gathering place. A shared room in a divided city. It was never strictly Catholic or Protestant. It was public. And public places in Belfast were dangerous places.

The pub sits directly across from the Europa Hotel—the most bombed hotel in Europe—and near Great Victoria Street station, a high-profile location that made it a soft but symbolic target. It was hit multiple times, part of the collateral damage in a war of identities, ideologies, and endurance.

What's notable is that the Crown was—and still is—considered neutral ground. It didn't fly flags. It didn't wear allegiances. It poured pints.

Guinness never made a statement about the Crown's bombings. Nor about the Troubles. The brewery stayed quiet, culturally neutral, and kept pouring in pubs on both sides of the divide. And somehow, that silence carried weight. A pint of Guinness became one of the few rituals both communities could share without accusation.

THE GAME, THE PINT, AND THE LINE

If you spend enough time in an Irish pub — in Ireland or anywhere the Irish gather — the GAA (Gaelic Athletic Association) is never far from the conversation. The games—Gaelic football, hurling and camogie—are a rhythm that stitches together seasons, villages, counties, and even continents. Ken, Barry's friend from Limerick, lives in that rhythm. His words are steeped in it:

> *Guinness for many fuels the GAA conversation off the field. It inspires the stories. It strengthens the GAA social bond. It, along with the pub, provides the platform for social interaction around the game, the result, the referee etc.*

Ken's played in four countries — Ireland, the U.S., Australia, England — and knows the taste of a pint after a match isn't just about stout, it's about shared effort, community, pride, and tradition. And when it comes to the match itself, he's clear about keeping the game the focus:

> *The absence of alcohol in the stands allows for the preservation of the game itself as a unique focal point. All the focus is on the 70 minutes of sporting entertainment. This heightens the excitement of having 'a few' after the match.*

He also sees Guinness's corporate presence not as intrusion but as part of the fabric:

> *The Guinness sponsorship of GAA merges and connects sport with the essence of Irish social life — the pub, the craic, the game. It positively supports the 0.0 brand.*

And whether the scoreboard reads win or loss, his ethos is the same:

> *There is one rule – celebrate and engage in both victory AND defeat.*

At Boland's, that tradition flows in more ways than one. Gareth, who helps out behind the bar now and then, pours a pint with the same focus he brings to coaching GAA football and hurling. He's got a coach's awareness — eyes on the whole field, or in this case, the whole room. You start to think about another round and there he is, across the bar, nodding and already on it. Under his guidance, the local GAA teams — still young — have already made their mark, winning or reaching their regional finals.

Ken and Gareth share the same sport but come to it from different lines on the map. Ken's home ground is Limerick, deep in the Republic. Gareth's is a village in the North — not "Northern Ireland," as he's quick to point out, but *the North of Ireland*. One night, during the band's break, I tried to pin that down, to understand exactly where. I drew the familiar border in the air, pointing below for the Republic and above for Northern Ireland. Gareth pointed just above the line and said:

> *This is my home… above this imaginary so-called border.*

It wasn't anger, it wasn't confusion — it was something more deliberate, a choice in how he names himself and where he belongs.

That's the other field the GAA plays on — not just the grass between goalposts, but the symbolic terrain of identity. The same game that unites Limerick and the North also carries different histories, loyalties, and ways of speaking about home. In the stands, Ken sees the absence of alcohol as part of preserving the family focus, the integrity of the match. Gareth sees the same ethos in his coaching — the discipline, the pride, the respect for what happens on the field. And afterward, for both men, the pint is where the stories come alive.

Guinness sits at the center of all this — as sponsor, as social glue, as cultural marker. For Ken, it's the platform for post-match storytelling and the social bond that follows victory or defeat. For Gareth, it's part of the unspoken choreography of community — the nod, the pour, the shared knowing that in this place, among these people, both the GAA and the Guinness are more than they first appear.

SYMBOLS IN STONE AND STOUT

To this day, there's no public record that Guinness or its parent company, Diageo, contributed financially to Belfast's post-conflict redevelopment. No funds for rebuilding, no official partnerships with peace organizations or public infrastructure projects. The Guinness family's philanthropic legacy—through the Iveagh Trust and other charities—focused on Dublin. They built housing, parks, cathedrals, and social institutions there. But their reach never extended north.

That legacy remained local.

So did the silence.

And yet, the pint endured. The Crown kept serving it. The snug kept holding it. And people—locals, tourists, the weary and the hopeful—kept ordering it.

Because sometimes, showing up matters.

Guinness never claimed to fix Belfast. It didn't rebuild its streets or bridge its politics. But it stayed. It poured. And in a place where everything else was contested, it was one of the few things everyone could still agree on.

Across Northern Ireland, the story repeats. In Derry's Waterside, even as murals in the Bogside spoke of sorrow and anger, locals ducked into pubs like The Ritz for a pint of Guinness—concerned more about the foam than the politics. It wasn't defiance. It was endurance. And on the other side of the river, bars like Peadar O'Donnell's echoed with music and laughter again—speakers spilling folk tunes as pints hit the bar.

Michaela served me a pint one night smiling, talking about what Guinness means to her. She recalled that the best Guinness she ever had was at The Harbour Bar, a tiny place overlooking Downings Bay in Donegal, but whenever she is back home in Derry, that *"there's no better place to have a pint and good craic than at Peadar O'Donnell's."* The smile never left her eyes, and I could tell as she was talking, she was right back there—transported back to the simpler times in her memory that carry on in an unsuspecting pint a continent away.

In County Antrim, centuries-old pubs like Ballycastle's House of McDonnell poured the same stout that had survived bombs and barricades. Guinness was everywhere—not a banner, not a protest, just reliable. It didn't broker peace, but it never left a room divided by flags.

Guinness doesn't fix history. But it holds it. And holds people long enough to sit, to reflect, to stay at the table just a little longer.

And maybe—someday—the rift will close. Not by decree. Not by referendum. But slowly, quietly, pint by pint. And perhaps when it does, Guinness will not only be the drink they both poured, but the example they both followed.

The pint doesn't take sides. But it lets people sit down long enough to remember they've both got a story.

8 THE SHADOW BENEATH THE FOAM

First you take a drink, then the drink takes a drink,
then the drink takes you.
—F. Scott Fitzgerald

The stories we tell over a pint are not always easy. Beneath the warmth and ritual, there are truths we've learned to swallow—histories of pain, addiction, and silence that deserve the same reverence we give to celebration.

There's a weight to a pint glass that goes beyond its ounces.

It rests heavy in the hand, yes, but also in the psyche—especially when that pint is Guinness, and the setting is Irish. At Boland's, where stories swirl as richly as the stout itself, you hear the laughter, the music, the clink of glasses. But between the verses of folk songs and the roar of a Six Nations match, there's a quieter truth humming underneath. One that rarely surfaces in toasts, but exists just the same.

This chapter isn't an indictment. It's an invitation—to see the whole picture. To look beneath the foam.

THE PINT AS TOTEM

In Ireland and its diaspora, Guinness isn't just a drink. It's a ritual. A badge. A backdrop. The first pint poured on arrival and the last sip taken before a farewell. It's the center of wakes, weddings, birthdays, and Tuesdays. For many, it's a marker of cultural pride. A liquid thread connecting Dingle to Dorchester, Donegal to the Bronx.

But reverence can sometimes blind us to responsibility. It's easy to forget, amid the elegance of a cascading pour, that alcohol—any alcohol—is a substance of consequence.

THE INHERITED STIGMA

The image of the "drunken Irishman" has been exported almost as widely as Guinness itself. Caricatured in movies, cemented in stereotypes, and absorbed into self-identity in ways both ironic and insidious. It's a stereotype weaponized by outsiders—and sometimes internalized by insiders.

Historically, the pub served a purpose. In rural Irish life, it was the hearth, the meeting hall, the courthouse of casual judgment. And in the Irish-American immigrant story, the bar often became the first business owned, the first refuge in a foreign land.

In this light, it's easy to see why the pint was more than a drink. It was safety. Autonomy. Belonging.

But that legacy is two-sided. In many families, it was also the source of fear. Of silence. Of inherited trauma.

TOWARD A DIFFERENT KIND OF LEGACY

Today, things are changing.

Guinness 0.0 ("Guinness Zero") is no longer a whisper but a choice proudly ordered. Sobriety is being rebranded, not as lack, but as empowerment. Groups like Alcohol Action Ireland, the Guinness Foundation, and others are funding initiatives for mental health, addiction recovery, and cultural transformation.

At Boland's, you'll sometimes see a group of friends ordering a round of zeros. No one bats an eye. The ritual remains. The intent has shifted.

Guinness 0.0 isn't a novelty. It's a fully brewed pint. It starts the same way as the classic Guinness Draught: water, barley, hops, and yeast. It's fermented, conditioned, matured. All of it. Only after the full brewing process does something else happen—something carefully engineered not to change the taste.

The alcohol is removed using a cold filtration method, a membrane-based process that filters out the alcohol molecules without heating the beer or damaging the flavor.[33] That's crucial. Because Guinness knows what the pint means. It's not just about what's in it—it's about what it evokes. The ritual. The rhythm. The creamy surge and settle. And if you mess with that, you've lost more than just alcohol.

---

[33] "Revealed: The secret process to remove alcohol from Guinness 0.0..." — Daily Mail, May 2024. https://www.dailymail.co.uk/news/article-13879035

The result is a beer that drinks like Guinness—full body, familiar mouthfeel, bitter dark roast, that soft, cascading head—but clocks in at 0.0% ABV.[34] It's available in widget cans on store shelves, and increasingly on draught in pubs across Ireland. In places like Boland's, it shows up in the same glass, at the same tables, poured with the same care.

It often costs just as much—or more—than its alcoholic counterpart, something that's raised eyebrows. But Guinness stands by the pricing. The process is specialized, and the intention is preservation. Not just of taste, but of belonging.

Because for some, the pint has to be alcohol-free. But that doesn't mean it can't still mean something.

VOICES FROM THE EDGE OF THE GLASS

Ireland has long told stories in song and silence—and some of the most powerful voices have come from those who've stood right at the edge of the glass.

Christy Moore gave it up. The iconic folk singer, raised on sessions and storytelling, walked away from alcohol in 1987. Not with fanfare, but with resolve.

Moore would openly discuss his relationship with drink as far back as 1991 in an interview for *The Daily Telegraph.*

---

[34] Official Guinness 0.0 Product Page https://www.guinness.com/en-us/beers/guinness-0

I had to drink to exist, drink to work, drink to think, drink to talk, drink to drink.[35]

Sobriety didn't mute him—it sharpened him. His presence in the pub became a symbol of something new: the ritual without the ruin, the song without the slur.

Shane MacGowan, by contrast, never stepped back. He stepped further in. The Pogues lead singer turned the wreckage into rhythm, becoming the patron saint of the half-smashed poet. For a time, it worked. His verses were jagged and holy. But the myth swallowed the man.

When he died in 2023, *The Daily Mail* summed his battle this way:

MacGowan faced a very public battle with alcohol and drug addiction. He started drinking when he was a young child at his family home in Ireland which he described as like 'living in a pub'. He once said that he hadn't been sober for a single day since he was 14.[36]

---

[35] Colin Randall, "Christy Moore interviewed: A Terrible Beauty and a 'privileged life,'" Salut! Live, October 31, 2024, https://www.salutlive.com/2024/10/christy-interview-will-do-it-up-for-posting-just-before-album-release-nov-1.html (accessed July 26, 2025).

[36] Isabelle Stanley, "Shane MacGowan's Life Through Quotes: 12 Unforgettable One-Liners from the Pogues Rocker about Drinking, Women, and Breaking Into America," Daily Mail, November 30, 2023, https://www.dailymail.co.uk/news/article-12809941/Shane-MacGowans-life-quotes-Pogues.html (accessed August 23, 2025).

Ireland mourned—but it also quietly asked itself what price is paid when the pint becomes performance.

And then there's Colin Farrell—the modern Irishman, Hollywood-polished but full of old-country ghosts. Once a tabloid darling, now sober and quietly self-possessed, he reframed his journey not as recovery, but as return.

During the Dublin International Film Festival in 2021, he would recount:

> *After 15 or 20 years of carousing the way I caroused and drinking the way I drank, the sober world is a pretty scary world... To come home and not to have the buffer support of a few drinks just to calm the nerves, it was a really amazing thing*[37].

He doesn't deny the past. He just lives differently now—proof that you can carry Irishness without carrying the weight of every myth.

These voices don't tell us to reject the pint. But they remind us: we must see it clearly. We must pour it with both hands—one holding reverence, the other holding responsibility. Because whether you raise a glass, set it

---

[37] Tanya Sweeney, "Colin Farrell: 'After 20 Years of Drinking the Way I Drank, the Sober World Is Pretty Scary,'" Irish Times, March 4, 2021, https://www.irishtimes.com/culture/film/colin-farrell-after-20-years-of-drinking-the-way-i-drank-the-sober-world-is-pretty-scary-1.4501552 (accessed August 23, 2025).

aside, or never touch it at all, *the ritual should serve the story—not the other way around.*

THE HELP THAT POURS BEYOND THE PINT

For all its weight and meaning, Guinness has never claimed to be a cure. And while it has built homes, funded cathedrals, supported the arts, and transformed the Irish working class with wages and welfare, it has not, historically, extended that same support to those whose lives were undone by the very drink it perfected.

The Guinness family gave Dublin dignity—housing through the Iveagh Trust, public health reforms, libraries, and parks. They pioneered corporate benevolence before the term existed. But their legacy, as sweeping as it was, did not include addiction treatment. They helped make drinking safer, cleaner, more honorable. But they did not speak to what happens when the pint no longer serves celebration, but escape.

Even today, under the modern Guinness brand, now part of Diageo, efforts around alcohol harm have taken shape—but only at the edges. DrinkIQ offers tools and education to help people make informed decisions. In Ireland, the company supports Drinkaware, a public messaging campaign aimed at moderation and responsibility. But these initiatives stop just short of the point where most damage lives—where dependency begins, and control fades. They educate, but they don't catch.

Instead, the burden of recovery rests elsewhere. It rests with nonprofit clinics, social workers, community programs, and volunteers. In Ireland, it's organizations working to change policies. It's the quiet, underfunded centers where someone might walk in after a hard night, asking for help instead of another pint. And across the Atlantic, in the Irish bars and neighborhoods of America, its community health providers, recovery counselors, and anonymous groups who meet in church basements beneath the stained-glass gaze of saints who've seen it all.

These are the people who meet the pint on the other side. Who step in when ritual becomes repetition, and repetition becomes risk.

And all of this lands differently when the story is your own.

I didn't grow up thinking of alcohol as dangerous. I understood it the way most people do: as a part of the background, an expected guest at the table. But in college, someone in my family mentioned—casually, almost offhandedly—that my grandmother had been an alcoholic.

She died when I was eight.
I hadn't known.
I hadn't even thought to ask.

But once I heard it, the shape of things began to change. The silences made more sense. The absences in memory, the sense that something had been there and not-there, became clearer.

No one brought it up again. It wasn't a scandal. It was simply part of the story I hadn't been told.

But it planted something in me—a pause.

A caution I still carry. Not fear, but awareness. A kind of alertness that hums in the background whenever I order a pint. I enjoy the ritual. I honor the pour. But I am always aware of the line.

That's what this chapter holds for me—not a rejection of the pint, but a reckoning with all it contains. The celebration. The connection. The legacy. But also the cost. The shadow. The truth we rarely toast.

We can still raise our pints. Still tell stories. Still find meaning in shared spaces and quiet songs. But we can also name what's beneath the foam—so that the ritual stays rooted in presence, not pretense. So that it lifts what matters, and lets go of what doesn't. So that what we pour still serves us. Not the other way around.

. . .

Important Note:

A list of support resources is included in the appendix and online at www.pintsandpower.com/alcohol-support for anyone who may need it.

9 BEYOND BUSINESS – THE GUINNESS FAMILY LEGACY

"They gave more than wages. They gave dignity."
– Iveagh Trust commemorative plaque

Clarity, in Ireland, often begins with legacy. Long before Guinness became a global symbol or cultural shorthand, it was a family name—one that left behind schools, housing, parks, and proof that business could build more than wealth.

THE FAMILY BEHIND THE NAME

From the very first day in 1759 until his death 44 years later, Arthur Guinness oversaw the daily workings of St. James's Gate with vision and resolve. In the centuries that followed, his descendants—sons and daughters, husbands, and wives—did more than carry on his name. They built a legacy of public purpose, reshaping Ireland and the wider world through beer, yes, but also through philanthropy, politics, culture, and care.

Most people know the name Guinness because of what's poured into a pint. But behind that black stout and creamy head is a family whose influence stretches far beyond brewing vats and pub taps. They built cathedrals, funded housing, preserved heritage, hosted salons, held public office, and at times stood at the very crossroads of history.

The Guinness family wasn't just a dynasty of businesspeople. They were architects of modern Irish and Anglo-Irish society—a blend of capitalists, stewards, reformers, and cultural catalysts. And while revolutions raged, the Guinnesses often worked quietly but deliberately, shaping policy, sustaining institutions, and improving the lives of workers and communities.

If they had stopped there—creating social benefits decades ahead of their time—that alone would have been remarkable. But they didn't stop.

They did much, much more—and not always in the ways history textbooks expect. Sometimes their power was held in public office. Sometimes it was poured quietly at a garden party, handwritten in a checkbook, or pressed into a heritage stone.

This is their chapter. Not just the brewers. The builders. The patrons. The revolutionaries of continuity.

ARTHUR GUINNESS & OLIVIA WHITMORE: THE FOUNDER AND THE FOUNDATION

Before there was a brewery, there was a marriage. When Arthur Guinness signed the lease at St. James's Gate in 1759, he was already married to Olivia Whitmore, a woman whose name rarely appears in historical footnotes, yet whose role was quietly monumental. Olivia would bear 21 children (10 of whom survived to adulthood)—a feat that, in 18th-century Ireland, was both biologically perilous and logistically extraordinary.

He built a brewery. She built the family that carried it.

Arthur Guinness (1725–1803) founded more than a business—he planted a cultural root system. As a Protestant in a Catholic-majority Ireland, he held unorthodox views for his time: reportedly supporting Catholic emancipation, religious tolerance, and Irish industry. He brewed not for the aristocracy, but for the people.

His vision, however, did not ferment in isolation. While Arthur carved out permanence in a country defined by instability, Olivia Whitmore Guinness stabilized the household from which the dynasty grew. She managed the family during Ireland's political unrest and economic hardship. She was not merely the mother of Arthur II—she was the matriarch of a brewing legacy.

In the Guinness story, Arthur may have signed the 9,000-year lease—but Olivia was the first guarantor of generational continuity. In a time when women had no legal power or political platform, her role as mother, steward, and silent partner made her an indispensable figure in the launch of one of Ireland's most influential families.

Her power was not in titles, but in endurance. Not in speech, but in structure.

ARTHUR GUINNESS II & ELIZABETH GUINNESS: THE EXPANSIONISTS IN SHADOW AND STEAM

If Arthur laid the foundation, it was Arthur Guinness II (1768–1855) who scaled it to a national force. He transformed the brewery into a full industrial operation—moving away from ale and fully committing to porter, which would become Guinness's defining product. During his stewardship, the brewery more than doubled in size, its reputation began reaching beyond Dublin, and employment expanded rapidly.

But expansion brought scrutiny. Whispers circulated that the Guinness family did not descend from the Irish Magennis clan at all but from a Cromwellian soldier who had stayed behind after conquest. Arthur II fought the charge fiercely, insisting on Irish lineage, knowing how quickly Dubliners could brand the family as more English than Irish. In defending the family name, he revealed the paradox that would follow the Guinness legacy: rooted in Ireland, accused of England, and destined to straddle both.

Yet this rise—from master brewer to industrialist—was accompanied by another quiet presence: his wife, Elizabeth Guinness (née Guinness). While the historical record says little of her, the silence is telling. In 19th-century Ireland, a woman like Elizabeth would have been the architect of social respectability, the manager of domestic and financial order, and the steward of future generations.

He built the engine. She kept the fire burning.

While Arthur II managed scale, Elizabeth likely managed legacy. She raised Benjamin Lee Guinness, whose civic vision would reshape Dublin. She held the household together through the Act of Union (1801) and the rising tensions between Irish industry and British governance. She also helped forge the family's identity as more than brewers—as citizens.

In the Guinness lineage, Elizabeth represents the moment when maternal labor became dynastic investment. She worked in the private sphere—but for a very public future.

BENJAMIN LEE GUINNESS & ISABELLA: THE BUILDER AND THE QUIET PILLAR

When Benjamin Lee Guinness (1798–1868) inherited the business, he didn't just expand it—he made it monumental. Under his leadership, Guinness became the largest brewery in Ireland, and arguably in the world. Yet his greatest legacy wasn't brewed—it was built. Benjamin personally funded the restoration of St. Patrick's Cathedral, then in ruin, as a gift to the people of Dublin. He also donated heavily to the improvement of city sanitation and water infrastructure, often at his own expense.

But Benjamin also embodied the contradictions of his family. He became the first Guinness to sit in the House of Commons as a Member of Parliament, tying the name to Westminster and the British establishment. At the same time, he gave Ireland one of its most enduring cultural symbols: the harp, emblazoned on every label of Guinness stout. And though his restoration of St. Patrick's Cathedral was an act of civic pride, it was a Protestant cathedral, not Catholic—an offering that could be read as both deeply Irish and firmly aligned with the Protestant Ascendancy. His public works, like his politics, revealed the paradox: loyal to England yet rooted in Dublin, elite in status yet gifting the city with its most Irish of symbols.

He didn't run for power. He rebuilt it in stone.

Behind this public force was Isabella Guinness (née Gresley)—his wife, moral compass, and stabilizing presence. Living through the Great Famine (1845–1852) and its aftermath, Isabella managed a growing household and helped project the kind of stability that gave Benjamin the freedom to act. Though she left little in the written record, her role would have mirrored the Victorian-era ideal of domestic philanthropy: managing charitable giving through religious and civic groups, stewarding household hospitality, and ensuring moral continuity.

She raised Edward Cecil Guinness, instilling in him the ethical and philanthropic frameworks that would define the Iveagh Trust and a new era of civic-minded Guinness leadership.

In Isabella's time, the role of women in power was never spoken—but it was always known. Hers was the quiet power that made public generosity credible.

EDWARD CECIL GUINNESS & ADELAIDE: THE ARCHITECT AND THE ALLY

Edward Cecil Guinness (1847-1927) inherited more than a brewery—he inherited a city on the edge of upheaval. By the time he became the dominant force at St. James's Gate in the late 1800s, Dublin was swelling with workers, starved for housing, and seething with inequality. Edward didn't just industrialize; he institutionalized dignity. He brought scale not only to production, but to philanthropy, founding the Iveagh Trust in 1890 to provide safe, permanent, clean housing for Dublin's working class.

But his stewardship was also marked by contradiction. In 1886, Edward floated Guinness on the London Stock Exchange and shifted its headquarters across the Irish Sea, cementing the family's place among Britain's financial aristocracy. Yet within a few short years, he poured much of his fortune back into Dublin, rebuilding the Liberties around St. James's Gate with housing blocks, public baths, and new sanitation systems. The same man who rooted the company in London's empire became the benefactor who remade Dublin's poorest streets.

He inherited a brewery and built a better Dublin.

Where his father restored cathedrals, Edward built public baths, libraries, and science endowments. He gave anonymously, generously, and strategically—blending aristocratic discretion with a civic conscience. At his death, his giving had exceeded £1 million, an unprecedented figure for private philanthropy in Ireland at the time.

But none of it happened in a vacuum.

Enter Adelaide Guinness, born Cavendish-Bentinck—a woman of impeccable English aristocratic lineage. Her marriage to Edward merged two powerful lineages: the Irish industrial magnate and the British landed elite. Yet she was more than a ceremonial figure. Adelaide brought with her not only the expectations of empire, but the tools to navigate it: a salon sensibility, social fluency, and a finely tuned grasp of how reputations were built in drawing rooms as much as boardrooms.

While Edward poured millions into homes and hospitals, Adelaide hosted the teas, organized the galas, and managed the social architecture that made such giving respectable, persuasive, and imitable. She helped translate Edward's Irish-rooted generosity into Anglo-Irish influence—the kind that allowed Guinness to navigate both Dublin's working class and London's political elite without contradiction.

In an age where Victorian women were expected to exert soft power, Adelaide mastered it. She wasn't behind Edward; she was beside him, facing a different direction— toward the society whose favor would shape the family's reach for decades to come.

She helped construct the unspoken message that made Guinness unique:

You may find us in your ledger books. But you'll respect us for what we build outside them.

RUPERT GUINNESS & GWENDOLEN: THE CHANCELLOR AND THE PARLIAMENTARIAN

If Edward Cecil Guinness raised the family's public conscience, his son Rupert Guinness, 2nd Earl of Iveagh (1874–1967) gave it intellectual and institutional weight. As a brewer, Rupert took a more reserved role in the business, but as Chancellor of the University of Dublin, Member of Parliament, and agricultural innovator at the Elveden Estate, he steered the Guinness name into the arenas of science, education, and food security.

Rupert helped shape wartime logistics and post-war planning, focusing on nutrition and land reform. During World War I, he was deeply involved in organizing food production and distribution in Britain and Ireland, and he was a proponent of applied science for public good.

But the most striking feature of this generation may not be Rupert at all—it's Gwendolen Guinness, Countess of Iveagh, who broke centuries of Guinness tradition by stepping into formal political office.

He served in chambers. She sat in Parliament.

Gwendolen (née Onslow) was elected as Conservative MP for Southend in 1927, succeeding Rupert in the seat when he inherited his title. She became one of the first female Members of Parliament in the UK and served until 1935, an extraordinary tenure at a time when women's political participation was still viewed as a novelty.

While Rupert embodied the aristocratic scholar, Gwendolen stood as a symbol of modern governance and public visibility. She campaigned actively, held surgeries for constituents,[38] and represented a new face of Guinness service: one that didn't just write checks but helped write policy.

---

[38] **"Surgeries"** in this context refers to scheduled meetings where a Member of Parliament meets privately with constituents to hear concerns, offer advice, or provide assistance on public or personal matters—akin to local office hours in U.S. politics.

In many ways, she embodied the shift from salon to statehouse—a Guinness woman not just shaping influence, but wielding it directly.

The quiet dynasty had found a voice—and it was hers.

BENJAMIN GUINNESS & MIRANDA: THE QUIET ESTATE AND ITS KEEPER

By the mid-20th century, the Guinness name had already become an institution—but with that stature came a shift in tone. Benjamin Guinness, 3rd Earl of Iveagh (1937–1992), inherited not only the Elveden estate but a legacy steeped in brewing, politics, and philanthropy. Yet unlike his forebears, Benjamin governed with discretion, more estate manager than public reformer.

While he did not hold elected office, his work continued the family's agricultural innovation and environmental stewardship at Elveden. He modernized operations, supported local initiatives, and remained a quiet but steady trustee of the Iveagh Trust, ensuring its mission endured through the social upheavals of the 1960s–80s.

At his side was Miranda Guinness (née Smiley)—a woman of equanimity and reserve, who embodied the waning traditions of aristocratic hospitality. Though less public than her predecessor Gwendolen, Miranda remained a visible patron of cultural and local philanthropic events, particularly in Suffolk.

His legacy wasn't loud. It was lived.

Miranda's role was emblematic of many aristocratic women in the post-war era: a curator of continuity. As society tilted toward egalitarianism, she helped preserve the family's sense of dignified duty without ostentation—maintaining the Elveden estate as a site of tradition, employment, and quiet Irish-English heritage.

EDWARD, RORY & CORY GUINNESS: THE PRESENT LEGACY AND LIVING LINE

The Guinness family has always been a conversation between the past and the future—and in this generation, that dialogue continues through three interlinked voices: a peer, a civic steward, and an heir.

Edward Guinness, 4th Earl of Iveagh (b. 1969), inherited his title young and has carried it with the quiet discipline that now defines the family's modern identity. Educated at Eton and serving as a Crossbench peer in the House of Lords, Edward is also the current steward of the Elveden Estate, a model of sustainable agriculture and heritage preservation. He remains closely tied to environmental causes and public duty, though he has stepped back from day-to-day philanthropy in Ireland.

That civic presence is now held by his brother, Rory Guinness (b. 1966), who today serves as the Chair of the Iveagh Trust—the very institution their great-great-grandfather founded to provide housing and dignity to Dublin's working class. Rory lives in Ireland and represents the branch of the family still rooted in the day-to-day reality of Irish civic life. In 2025, Rory published *World of Guinness*, a personal and cultural reflection on the family's values, reach, and responsibility across generations—a resource that richly informs this chapter perhaps best summed up by these closing remarks of that chapter.

There are clear links between the philanthropic
activities of different generations of the family, which
have been undertaken entirely in a personal capacity,
away from commercial life of the brewery.... I am
pleased to say that this generation's commitment to
Dublin is ongoing.[39]

Together, the brothers represent a bifurcated legacy:
Edward continues the aristocratic presence in Britain, while
Rory maintains the family's moral and civic inheritance in
Ireland.

And then there is the next chapter: Cory Guinness (b. 1996),
Edward's son and the heir apparent. A former Royal Marine
officer and equerry to Queen Elizabeth II, Cory has already
walked the corridors of monarchy and military—two
institutions long entwined with the Guinness legacy. He
stands as a modern emblem of the family's enduring values:
discipline, public service, and discretion.

In this generation, the Guinnesses no longer shape policy—
but they still shape lives. Through housing, heritage, land,
and quiet leadership, Edward, Rory, and Cory reflect a
legacy not of power seized, but of responsibility carried.

Some dynasties end in the pages of history.
This one writes its story in the lives of others.

---

[39] Rory Guinness. *World of Guinness*, p. 67.

ECHOES OF THE LINEAGE:
GUINNESSES BEYOND THE GATE

The Guinness dynasty did not flow solely through the main artery of Arthur's descendants at St. James's Gate. Over the centuries, other branches flourished—sometimes more flamboyantly, sometimes more controversially—but always with the unmistakable gravity of the name. These were the Guinnesses who expanded the family imprint into politics, preservation, poetry, and even pop culture.

Walter Guinness, brother of Rupert, later Lord Moyne, took the family name deep into the machinery of the British Empire. As Minister of State in the Middle East during World War II, he became both architect and lightning rod of British colonial policy. His assassination in Cairo in 1944 by Zionist militants marked a dramatic and bloody punctuation in Britain's withdrawal from empire—proof that even the quieter Guinnesses found themselves in the eye of history.

His son, Bryan Guinness), was less interested in politics and more in poetry. A novelist and patron of the arts, he married the luminous and soon-to-be-notorious Diana Mitford— later one of the fascist-aligned Mitford sisters. Their union, brief and brilliant, pulled the Guinness name into the orbit of literary salons and political scandal, and then out again.

From culture's edges to its preservationists, there was Desmond Guinness, a descendant who in 1958 co-founded the Irish Georgian Society, a conservation organization dedicated to preserving Ireland's Georgian architecture and decorative heritage. Where others built factories or bought titles, Desmond preserved buildings: Palladian townhouses, country estates, and classical facades that would have vanished from Irish skylines without his stubborn aestheticism. He spoke of heritage the way his ancestors spoke of hops and barley—with care, conviction, and civic pride.

And then there was Tara Browne—a comet rather than a steward. Born to Oonagh Guinness, herself part of the "Golden Guinness Girls" who with sisters, Alieen and Maureen were daughters of Rupert's brother Earnest. Tara embodied Swinging London in the 1960s. When he crashed his car at age 21, it wasn't just the loss of a scion—it was the closing of a chapter in youthful aristocratic bohemia. Immortalized by The Beatles in *"A Day in the Life"*—"He blew his mind out in a car"—Tara became the Guinness who entered global myth through a melody, not a deed.

Even in the present, the constellation expands. Patrick Guinness, historian and genealogist, quietly continues the work of stitching together Ireland's past.

Sabrina Guinness, television producer and modern matriarch of sorts, has danced between charity, celebrity, and cultural influence in Britain.

Each of them stands slightly outside the central Guinness current—but they all reflect the same light. Their paths diverge, but their orbits remain steady: shaping society, stewarding memory, and proving that one family can hold both lineage and legacy in delicate, generational balance.

WHAT THEY GAVE IRELAND
(WITHOUT TAKING CREDIT)

From Arthur's first signature on that 9,000-year lease to Cory's quiet step into a future not yet written, each generation left something behind: housing, dignity, policy, memory, myth. And woven among the ledgers and trusts were the women—wives, mothers, leaders—who ensured the legacy would last not just in names, but in values.

They helped Ireland survive—not just economically, but culturally and spiritually. They offered more than employment. They offered belonging—a sense that Irish lives were worth investing in, not despite their place in empire, but in defiance of it.

Without fanfare, they made continuity look like rebellion. They made power feel like stewardship. And in doing so, they gave Ireland—and the world—a new way to understand what legacy truly means.

Again and again, the Guinnesses crossed the line between Irish and English identities, between royalist elite and populist benefactor. Their legacy is not a simple arc but a constant crossing—a paradox that still shapes how the pint is remembered today.

10   THE POUR AND THE PLACE

"God invented whiskey to keep the Irish from ruling the world.
Guinness gave them a reason to gather anyway."
– Traditional joke

Connection doesn't happen by accident. It happens in places built for it—places like the Irish pub, where the pace slows, the pour matters, and the air between people fills with memory and meaning.

MORE THAN A BAR

Call it what you like—the public house, the local, the snug, the boozer. In Ireland, the pub is not just a place to drink.

It's a place to gather. To listen. To laugh. To grieve. To sing. To remember.

And in almost every pub, there's one common thread: Guinness. Not just because it's popular, but because it has become part of the performance of Irish life. You don't just drink it. You witness it. You participate in it.

THE THEATER OF THE POUR

There are few acts in modern life that are as ritualistic as the pouring of a Guinness.

This isn't a gimmick—it's a form of respect. Guinness Master Brewer Fergal Murray said it best.

No other beer has to go through ritual. We make the ritual important. It's theater. The ceremony behind pouring a pint is essential to the consumer's requirement for a perfect pint of Guinness. It's all part of the indefinable essence. The ritual and the crafting of the pint is about serving the beverage to your customer in the right way. With any other beer, you can just put it under the tap and hand it out. But with Guinness you've got to think about it.[40]

The clean tulip glass being held under the tap at the exact, perfect angle (45-degrees). The nitrogen surge, like smoke in reverse, and then the pause... the settle. The final top-up – pushing back, not pulling the tap. And there it is, what you've been so patiently awaiting - the signature dome of cream on darkness.

You wait. You don't rush it. You don't sip before it's ready. You watch.

To pour a Guinness properly is to say: "This moment matters. You matter."

And the pub, in its quiet way, reinforces that message.

---

[40] Yenne, *Guinness: The 250-Year Quest for the Perfect Pint*, xv.

THE PUB AS PUBLIC LIVING ROOM

Especially in rural Ireland, the pub serves the roles abandoned by formal institutions, there the pub is more than a place to drink—it's the town square where news travels faster than broadband, carried pint to pint across the low hum of local voices. It's the counselor's office, where grief is poured as gently as stout and solace comes in the form of silence or song. It's the music hall, where a fiddle tune or a whispered chorus can raise the rafters and lower the weight of a hard week. And it's the place where the weather isn't just small talk—it's philosophy. Rain isn't just rain; it's a metaphor for loss, a reason for reflection, a measure of memory.

In cities, the pub shifts shape. It becomes a stage for reinvention—a place where identities bend and blend, where stories from old counties and new beginnings echo off the walls and no one quite knows who walked in with what name. But they all leave with something shared: a sense, however fleeting, of having been seen, heard, and held in the amber glow of something older than explanation.

But no matter the setting, the pint defines the rhythm. It sets the pace. The two-part pour slows the world down, invites eye contact, creates space.

That rhythm isn't just felt in the pub. It shows up on screen, too—in the way Irish films and Irish-American portrayals so often center the pint without naming it. Think of *The Quiet Man* (1952). John Ford's sweeping, sentimental vision of the homeland may be drenched in myth, but in its pub scenes, it gets something quietly, perfectly right. The pints—never labeled—arrive slow, dark, and creamy. They're not props. They're part of the architecture of belonging. There's no need for the bartender to say "*Guinness*"—everyone already knows. The drink is assumed, absorbed into the ritual. It's what's poured when pride is wounded, when peace is brokered, or when nothing else needs to be said.

That's not marketing. That's culture.

GUINNESS AS A UNIFIER

Throughout Irish history—the pub has played a central role. As a meeting place. As living room. As political and social center. While sectarian establishments served those who lived in the neighborhood, pints of Guinness were served in both. A single point of common ground throughout the course turbulent decades.

No matter the side, while the definition of what being Irish meant may have been different, the famous black stout was part of that definition.

In the years surrounding the Good Friday Agreement, many publicans in Northern Ireland chose to keep their pubs neutral. Flags stayed down. Political debates were left at the door. But Guinness flowed.

A Protestant and a Catholic might now sit at opposite ends of the same room, and order the same pint.

Because Guinness doesn't declare sides.
It declares intention.

It says: "This is a place where the story can still unfold. This is where common ground can be found"

A modern example unfolded during the summer of 2024, a meeting between two leaders from different countries met. On July 17 of that year, Irish Taoiseach Simon Harris and new British Prime Minister Keir Starmer met over a shared pint of Guinness as a part of a pledge to work more closely together on topics of Northern Ireland and tensions around the wounds of Brexit.[41]

A PLACE TO REMEMBER AND CELEBRATE OUR HEROES AND GHOSTS

At Boland's, Shuggy has built a place where you can feel just as at home on your first pint as on your hundredth.

I've spent many a night, after last call, doors locked, the craic in full flow with music from The Coronas playing on YouTube. Special nights. Special people. The music filling the empty pub felt like it was just for us — a reminder that the same magic can happen whether you're shoulder to shoulder in a crowd or sitting in the quiet with a few friends and a last pint.

---

[41] Reuters, "British, Irish PMs seek to reset strained ties over pints of Guinness," Reuters.com, accessed May, 24, 2025, https://www.reuters.com/world/uk/british-irish-pms-seek-reset-strained-ties-over-pints-guinness-2024-07-17.

The Coronas are one of those Irish bands that can fill a stadium at home and still make a packed music hall feel like a neighborhood pub.

Frontman Danny O'Reilly, drummer Conor Egan, and bassist Graham Knox have been playing together since their college days in Dublin. The band are old friends of Shuggy's from back in those days, which makes it easy to picture him walking into Boland's and feeling instantly at home.

Their sound blends modern Irish rock with the kind of storytelling you'd expect to hear over a pint. At a Coronas show, the air feels charged — the crowd thick with Irish college kids, shoulder to shoulder, hoisting each other up as the tricolor comes out.

Then *Heroes or Ghosts* kicks in — slipping into a verse in Irish — and the place just lifts. It's the same current I've felt in a pub when the perfect pint lands in front of you: pride, memory, and belonging, all at once.

Danny stands at the center of it, carrying not just his own voice but the weight of a family steeped in music. His mother, Mary Black, has been one of the defining voices of Irish folk for decades. His sister, Róisín O, and cousin, Aoife Scott, carry that torch in their own ways.

Together, the three of them gifted the world with a version of *Grace* that can stop you in your tracks — the kind of song that makes the whole room go quiet, not because it has to, but because it wants to.

A PINT FOR EVERY MOOD

One of Guinness's greatest strengths is its range. It belongs to all kinds of moments.

A birthday calls for a raised pint, the head kissed before the first sip. A loss asks for a quiet one—no words needed, just the silence shared between glasses. A reunion brings clinks and laughter, the rhythm of reconnection. And sometimes, solitude itself asks for a single glass, one corner, one memory that hasn't yet faded.

Few drinks carry that kind of emotional bandwidth. Fewer still do it without announcing themselves. Barry, who spent years frequenting Tom Collins in Limerick, said it best:

> *Many quality conversations took place over a few pints in Tom Collins. It's a place where conversation flows freely—the more Guinness that is consumed, the more freely the conversation flows! ... In vino veritas—conversations are authentic and meaningful, where one's shyness and reluctance to engage fades into the background.*

That's the power of the pub—not just as a location, but as an emotional container. And that's what Guinness helps unlock. The words don't always come easy. But sometimes, with the right pint in the right place, they come exactly when they're needed.

11   THE RITUAL IN THE GLASS

"You don't just pour a Guinness. You prepare for it."
– Bartender's proverb

The pour is never just about the drink. It's about the reverence behind it. A proper Guinness doesn't just quench—it confirms. It reminds the drinker that they belong, and that someone thought they were worth the wait.

The shape. The settle. The silence. It all matters.

THE GLASS THAT CARRIES A NATION

You can recognize it from across the bar: the iconic tulip shape, the black body rising to a thick, creamy head, the harp just below the rim.

It's not just a glass. It's a signal.
Of place. Of pace. Of pride.

Other beers are poured.
Guinness is presented.

And every detail—its shape, its chemistry, its ritual—tells a story centuries in the making.

FROM BARREL TO NITROGEN: THE POUR EVOLVES

Originally, Guinness was drawn directly from wooden casks, using gravity taps or hand-pumps. There was no standardized pour. No ceremonial glass. Just stout, sometimes flat, sometimes frothy, always inconsistent.

The invention of nitrogenation in 1959 changed everything.

Developed to commemorate Guinness's 200th anniversary, this technique introduced a mixture of nitrogen (N_2) and carbon dioxide (CO_2) to the beer. Nitrogen's smaller bubbles and lower solubility created the signature velvety mouthfeel, the mesmerizing cascade during the settle and that durable, creamy head.

This innovation allowed Guinness to be poured with precision, served with reverence, and recognized instantly—anywhere in the world.

It turned the pint into a performance.

THE TWO-PART POUR: WHY WE WAIT

A proper Guinness is not rushed.

The two-part pour is as sacred as any ritual in Irish life:

The first pour: glass tilted, filled to just under the harp
The wait: 90 seconds of nitrogen doing its work
The top-off: a slow, vertical finish to form the perfect head

In total: 119.5 seconds.

Why the precision?

Because Guinness isn't just about flavor. It's about intention. To drink it properly, you must be present.

For Barry, a teacher and traveler raised in Dublin, that presence wasn't immediate—it arrived later in life, after a stretch in France and a return home. Guinness didn't start as something he loved. *"It was an adult thing to do,"* he recalled. The drink was heavier than others, more acquired than expected. And yet, something happened when he watched it being poured.

> *"I remember looking at the pint settle and the anticipation I felt in waiting to drink it,"* he said. *"It was almost ritualistic; the pour, the wait, the top up, the wait again and finally the sip!"*

It wasn't just the taste. It was the waiting. The ceremony. The patience required. Bartenders, he said, treated the pulling of a pint as *"almost a sacred act."* And for Barry, that reverence elevated the drink beyond preference. It became a moment that asked something of you in return: Stillness. Respect. Intention.

That's the heart of it. For many, Guinness doesn't just reward patience—it teaches it. The pour becomes a rite of passage not just culturally, but personally. It's where appreciation begins—not in the drinking, but in the watching. And the waiting.

There are places where the pint is the loudest thing in the room—and places where it's what lets people finally speak. The best pubs understand both. They hold your laughter when you're leaning into the band—and your silence when someone finally tells the story they've been holding for years.

That's why it's the drink of storytellers, thinkers, and those who value the moment.

THE SHAPE MATTERS

The tulip-shaped Guinness glass isn't just aesthetic. It's engineering.

The curve encourages nitrogen to surge upward in the center and cascade downward along the walls

The narrow mouth concentrates aroma

The flared top catches the head, creating that dome of foam without spillage

This isn't a container. It's a chamber of experience.

And people care. Deeply.

WHEN THEY CHANGED THE GLASS— THE WORLD NOTICED

In 2010, Guinness introduced a new pint glass for the first time in a decade. Taller, narrower, subtly contoured, and heavier in the hand, it featured an embossed 3D harp on the back and a shifted curvature designed to better hold the head and enhance the aroma. Branded as the "Gravity Glass," it was a quiet evolution of form with a calculated purpose: modernize the experience without disrupting the ritual.

To some, it wasn't even noticed.

But not to the faithful.

Irish forums lit up. Bartenders groaned. Regulars said their grip felt off. A few insisted the beer itself tasted different. And some, in quiet defiance, began requesting the old glass from behind the bar—out of habit, maybe, but more likely out of something deeper.

It wasn't about vanity.
It was about trust.

Guinness, they believed, wasn't supposed to change. Not in that way. The glass wasn't just packaging. It was part of the bond—the final frame in a ritual that had become sacred.

THE GLASS AS MEMORY

Guinness glassware tells stories, even when no one's speaking.

There are pint glasses saved from milestone birthdays, the date worn but the shape familiar. Commemorative editions from rugby tournaments or weddings, boxed and unboxed like heirlooms. Chipped ones tucked in cabinets—too meaningful to toss. Engraved ones passed between fathers and sons, names etched beside the harp like a quiet kind of legacy.

These aren't just drinking vessels. They're personal archives. Physical reminders of where we were, who we were with, and what was said—or left unsaid—between sips.

You don't collect Guinness bottles.
You collect Guinness moments.
And the glass remembers.

SPLITTING THE "G"

Not every ritual of the pint is solemn. Some are playful, precise, and tinged with the same quiet seriousness as the pour itself. For example, "Splitting the G," its ritual follows

1. **Start with a fresh pint of Guinness**: Ensure that the pint is poured correctly.

2. **Leave the pint to settle**: Wait for 60-90 seconds.

3. **Take a large, uninterrupted sip**: Take a large sip (you can gulp multiple times).

4. **Assess your result**: Place the pint on a flat, level surface (holding it is not okay).

   - **Goal**: The line between the beer and the creamy foam should stop in the gap within the G.

5. **Celebrate**: If you've done it correctly, you've successfully 'Split the G.'[42]

It's a ritual of attention, patience, and self-control. Friends tease each other about missing the mark. Bartenders smile

---

[42] Christopher Osburn, "How to Split the G: The Unofficial Rules of Guinness Golf," Man of Many, July 18, 2025, https://manofmany.com/culture/how-to-split-the-g-guinness (accessed August 22, 2025).

when someone lands it perfectly. A small thing, yes, but like all rituals, it says something about the relationship between the person and the pint. You're not just drinking Guinness— you're engaging with it, measuring yourself against it, finding joy in the balance.

The game is no myth—"Splitting the G" is played in pubs worldwide, as noted in guides and on social media, and even Guinness owner Diageo confirms that the true split lines up with the horizontal bars of the "G" and "E."

THE MIXED PINT

In every pub that pours Guinness, there's one conversation that never quite settles — the one about what belongs in the glass.

For some, a pint of Guinness is sacred. It's poured slowly, served pure, and never tampered with. The ceremony itself is the point — the weight of the glass, the stillness before the sip, the reverence in the wait. To alter that feels, to them, like rewriting a prayer.

And yet, there's another ritual — quieter, but no less deliberate — that takes place on bars across Ireland and beyond. It's the ritual of the *Half and Half*: that moment when a bartender, confident in their craft, balances gravity itself.

It starts with the base — the lighter ale or cider poured to the halfway mark, left to settle and breathe. Then comes the spoon... its curved back catching the flow so the dark stout settles gently atop the lighter ale.

There are many variations — each with its own personality. The *Black and Tan* pairs Guinness with pale ale, the most familiar version in the States, though in Ireland that name carries a darker echo of the British auxiliaries who terrorized civilians during the War of Independence. Out of respect, Irish bartenders simply call it a *Half and Half.* The *Blacksmith* blends Guinness with Smithwick's, a nod to Ireland's twin brewing traditions, while the *Snakebite* marries Guinness and cider — sweetness and stout, rebellion and ritual in the same glass. And the *Black Velvet,* once poured for royalty, floats Guinness atop champagne — a pairing of worker and aristocrat, solemnity and celebration.

Most people know the drinks without knowing their names. They just remember the sight — that clean divide of light beneath dark, the clean divide of light and dark, the way contrast becomes balance. Maybe that's part of the charm — these pints pull in those who aren't quite ready for the full dark yet.

It's not chaos. It's choreography. When done right, it holds its form like stained glass — two worlds in one glass that never quite blend but somehow belong together.

The purists might shake their heads. To them, Guinness should stand alone, unaccompanied. But others see something else — not a dilution of the ritual, but an evolution of it. A way for the Guinness novice to enter the conversation. A visual metaphor for the way Irishness itself has always been layered — the mingling of histories, cultures, and contradictions that somehow find harmony in contrast.

Because Guinness has always been about more than what's inside the glass. It's about the intent behind the pour — the patience, the care, the invitation. It's about the intent behind the pour — the patience, the care, the invitation.

Maybe the real beauty isn't in the purity of the pour, but in the line that separates one world from another — and still somehow connects them.

The layering spoon, chained to the bar, becomes a quiet symbol of that truth — that tradition can be tethered and shared at once. "The layering spoon, chained to the bar, becomes a quiet symbol of that truth — that tradition can be tethered and shared at once.

TOP SHELF, TOP RITUAL

At Boland's, there's a quiet ritual you won't find on the menu. It's not advertised, and most wouldn't even know it exists—unless they've earned it. I just call it the "*Top Shelf Glass Crew*," but if you know, you know: it's really called the "*An Cú Liath Alumni Club.*"

If you've spent any time in Massachusetts, you know we've got no shortage of Irish bars. Some have been pouring pints since your grandfather's day, others flash onto the scene and fade just as fast. Not far from where Boland's now stands, there was once a pub called The Grey Hound—or in Irish, *An Cú Liath*. It was owned by Paul and his wife, and for regulars like Kevin and Barefoot Scott, it wasn't just a pub—it was home. Scott is more like a brother to Paul than a teammate on the dartboard. When the Grey Hound closed, it hit hard.

Many of those who had a seat stitched into the rhythm of that place eventually found their way to Boland's. And with them, quietly, came the roots of a tradition.

From basements and kitchen cupboards, a collection of classic Guinness tulip glasses began to reappear. These weren't your standard barware. They were old-school— smooth, slightly shorter, with a wider bowl and a proper bulge in the middle. Some bore vintage Guinness logos. Others carried GAA crests or marked long-forgotten match days and family events. No two exactly alike, but all unmistakably right.

To the members of the crew, these glasses are non-negotiable. Their pints are only ever poured into them. They sit on the literal top shelf behind the bar—easy to spot, but only pulled down for a few. Not out of snobbery. Out of memory. Out of muscle. Out of respect.

And it's become a bit of a rite of passage for new staff. *"Let's see how long it takes before one of the crew gets a pint in the wrong glass,"* someone will whisper, pint in hand, a smirk just behind the foam.

Now and then, I'm lucky enough to be handed one. And I swear, the pint tastes different. Not just better—truer. Like it belongs to you. Or maybe, you belong to it.

Where the glasses originally came from is a bit of a myth. Some say they were liberated—one glass at a time—from unsuspecting pubs. Others believe they were quietly passed down, bequeathed by the Grey Hound faithful with one simple charge: *Hold these until the right place shows up.*

At one point—long before I understood any of this—I ended up with one of the glasses at home. It happens. But word travels fast. And once it did, I carried the weight of it like a confession.

On Father's Day 2024, I brought it back. Quiet afternoon, no fanfare. I placed it on the bar and offered it back to Kevin and Scott with the humility the moment deserved.

And right as I stepped back from the bar, my phone lit up. It was a FaceTime call from Ireland. My daughter, standing at the lake in Gougane Barra, smiling brighter than the water behind her. She'd just been engaged. I was still holding the bar when I heard the news.

When the call ended, Kevin bought the next pint. He asked for it to be poured it into that same glass—the one I had just returned, the one I didn't deserve but had brought home. And it settled perfectly. I snapped a photo of it. Not just to remember the pint—but to remember that moment.

That's the glass on the cover of this book.

Around the world, the Guinness ritual plays out ten million times a day. But not like this. Not like the *An Cú Liath* Alumni Club at Boland's. And yet, I'd wager there are others. Quiet clubs. Earned glasses. Familiar shelves holding more than just glassware—holding memory.

You don't ask to join. You just show up long enough, respect the pour, and one day someone slides the right glass your way.

And you know exactly what it means.

A PINT WITH MY NAME ON IT

I'll never forget standing behind the bar at the Guinness Storehouse, staring down at the tap with my name on the screen. I had signed up for the add-on experience—the "Perfect Pour." I was skeptical. I'd been through the tour. I knew the story. But now I was about to step into it.

They walked us through the two-part ritual—angle, settle, top-off—and handed each of us a clean tulip glass. When it was my turn, I poured slowly, nervously, reverently, watching the cascade like I'd watched it a hundred times before.

But this time, it wasn't just a pour. It was a kind of initiation.

When the head domed perfectly, the tap was closed, and I looked down at my pint—my own pour—I felt something surprisingly emotional. I was proud yet slightly dissatisfied with the result wanting to give it another try.

They handed me a certificate. A small thing. A novelty. But part of me believed it.

I was now, officially, part of the ritual.
Not just a drinker of Guinness.
A guardian of the pour.

TWO PINTS. TWO POURS.
TWO CONTINENTS. TWO DAYS.

In the summer of 2024, we spent our last night in Ireland at The Horse Shoe, a pub in the Crumlin area of Dublin, a working-class local that doesn't look like much from the outside—but like so many true Irish pubs, it opens into something deeper once you're inside. We were there to visit Bridie, Shuggy's mum. She's a legend. Still behind the bar, pouring perfect pints and making strangers feel like family.

She showed us the bar top—a jaw-dropping mosaic of thousands of beer caps she helped design and then painstakingly assembled cap by cap, then all seamlessly sealed in clear resin. The whole thing shimmered in the dim light, like the surface of a memory.

She poured perfect pints, beaming at each pull like it was the first time. We met regulars who welcomed us instantly—because we knew Bridie. And Shuggy. Or as they called him: Stephen.

At one point, Bridie waved me behind the bar and handed me the tap. *"Your turn,"* she said. I poured my own pint— slow, reverent, and under her watchful eye. It was an honor, plain and simple. That pour meant more than I expected.

Maybe it meant something more because of where we were: Crumlin. Not far from where Phil Lynott was born. He didn't just grow up Irish—he redefined what that meant. Black, rebellious, poetic, and unmistakably Irish, he rose from the streets of Dublin to international stardom with Thin Lizzy, rewriting the rules of rock and reclaiming Irishness on a global stage. And Crumlin never left him.

Once when asked about being black and Irish he quipped *"it's kinda like a pint of Guinness."*[43]

Dark. Complicated. But no less Irish.

He played his early gigs in pubs like this one—rooms full of sweat, sound, and stout. Guinness poured into those glasses like electricity into amplifiers. The pub was his stage, the people his pulse. Songs like *Whiskey in the Jar* and *The Boys Are Back in Town* weren't just anthems—they were a cultural reckoning. Stories of mates, misfits, and loyalty, poured out over pints.

It all came together in Crumlin. And somehow, I was pulling a pint where that current still lived.

Bridie told us stories that night—of hard times, stubborn hope, and her own history. The kind of truths that don't need polish. The kind you trust because of who's telling them.

The next day, we flew back to Boston. That same evening, I walked into Boland's.

Shuggy was there. So were the regulars. They cheered when I stepped in. *"We were just telling the story,"* someone said.

---

[43] "Kinda like a pint of Guinness," Writ in Water, April 14, 2015, https://writ-in-water.com/2015/04/14/kinda-like-pint-guinness (accessed June 21, 2025).

Shuggy had already heard. *"You pulled one at me mum's? Then you're pulling one here."*

And just like that, I was behind the bar again.
Two pints.
Two countries.
Thirty hours apart.

And someone shouted as I stepped out: *"The boys are back in town!"*

And maybe that's the thing. You can cross oceans. Leave and return. Be Irish by blood or by spirit. Be black and Irish. Be American and still pulled into something deeper. Because sometimes a pint isn't just a drink.

Sometimes, a pint is proof.

Proof that you belong.
Proof that memory can be shared.
Proof that the ritual doesn't need to be explained—only honored.

It's not just the pour.
It's what flows between people when it's poured right.

WHY IT STILL MATTERS

In a world of fast pours, Red Solo® cups, and digital noise, the Guinness glass remains analog, patient, and proud. It represents craftsmanship, commitment, a moment you're not willing to rush. It reminds us that what holds the thing can matter as much as the thing itself.

The glass is the frame.
The pour is the art.
The sip is the story.

And the wait is what makes it worthy. It can all be found in the ritual of the pour… and what follows.

if you're lucky and have found your true local—your living room away from home—where Guinness pours like a religion, then you will certainly end the night with *"just one more."*

Epilogue: A Pint with a Purpose

> *"Being Irish means remembering your roots*
> *and raising your glass."*
> – Irish diaspora toast

Every story leaves something behind. Not just facts or memories, but a feeling—of presence, of place, of something held longer than expected. The pint, when poured right, doesn't close the story. It invites its continuation, in every shared round, every quiet moment, and every return to the ritual that made it matter.

Sometimes belonging isn't inherited—it's poured.

WE CAME HOME, BUT WE BROUGHT IRELAND BACK WITH US

After our first trip to visit our daughter, we came back changed. And a few months later, we heard about a new Irish bar opening nearby. Small. Local. Run by a Dubliner named Shuggy. A rock musician once. A publican now.

We went—not for a drink, but for a feeling.
Not for the beer, but for the echo.

And when the pint arrived, and settled on the bar, I wasn't expecting much. But something in the way it was poured, placed, and presented—something in the silence that followed—brought it all back.

It wasn't about taste. It was about time.
Memory.
Meaning.
Home.

BOLAND'S, AND A POUR THAT SAID EVERYTHING

We kept going back. The pub became more than a novelty. It became a kind of bridge. The music. The people. The stillness. And always—Guinness.

Shuggy poured it like it mattered. Like it belonged to him. And in those moments, it belonged to me too.

We talked. We listened. I asked him what Guinness meant to him, and his answer wasn't rehearsed.

"It's home in a glass," he said. *"And a story in every pour."*

That's when I knew this wasn't just a drink.
It was a language.

And I wanted to speak it.

Maybe that's what made the next realization so satisfying. A few weeks after that night, it finally clicked—his last name.

Of course it was! The man who built a place where pouring Guinness is like a prayer... the one who taught me that the glass could carry identity, memory, and belonging... his name had been telling the story all along.

What is it?

Porter.

WHY I WROTE THIS BOOK

This book didn't come from a marketing brainstorm or a historical thesis. It came from that quiet moment at the bar, watching the pint settle, remembering the feel of cobblestones in Cork, hearing the echo of my daughter's voice when she said she'd found her place in the world.

It came from a deep, quiet belief that Guinness is not just history—it's present. It's personal.

It came from wanting to understand what this drink has carried over centuries. What it means to those who left. To those who stayed. To those who found it, like I did, not by birthright—but by recognition.

As I spread the word of my desire to do something with the idea, something meaningful, it was in the animated responses from everyone I told where I found my inspiration. When I started to share drafts that expressed common memories or moments, as more people started to talk about it to others, that's when it took on a life all of its own.

Even now, as I get ready to go to press, I'm experiencing my 15 minutes of fame in my own little circle. The work on the companion website pintsandpower.com is starting to gain followers and traction too.

It really is wonderful when someone you have known, but not known well, comes up to you and asks "Do you mind if I tell you a story about Guinness?" or "I can't wait to read the chapter about…" And the rest of your visit is spent at their table, invited in and no longer just acquaintances. It is for them… and for me that I wrote this book… and ultimately for you. Welcome to my bubble.

THE POUR THAT FINDS YOU

You don't have to be Irish to feel what Guinness means.

Barry put it best:

> We as Irish people don't have a monopoly on Guinness nor the feelings it conjures up for others. … They obviously have good taste! And in fairness, I have never met someone who doesn't love the Irish!

You just have to sit with it, wait for it, respect the ritual, and listen for the story in the glass. And when you do, something remarkable happens: you're no longer just holding a pint— you're holding belonging, quietly poured and patiently earned.

WHAT'S NEXT

There's more I want to explore—more to learn from Shuggy, from other publicans, from the people who keep this ritual alive. That's what the next chapter of this project will be.

But next chapters aren't just metaphor. They're real.

As I write this, we're preparing for our daughter's wedding in West Cork. And we're getting ready to send our youngest off for a year in Spain.

I never knew what Ireland would mean to me until I met it. Until it welcomed me in and offered something I didn't know I was missing. Who knows—maybe Spain has a story waiting too. Maybe there's a book about Sangria in my future.

But for now, all I can say is this:

Thank you, Ireland, for what you've poured into my life. And thank you, Guinness, for showing me that sometimes the truest things aren't shouted.

They're served.

Waited for.

And shared.

FIRST POUR
EDITION

APPENDIX A:

ALCOHOL RECOVERY AND HEALTH RESOURCES

The pint holds meaning. It connects, celebrates, and remembers. But for many, it also carries a weight—one that becomes too much to carry alone.

Whether you're reevaluating your relationship with alcohol, seeking help for someone you love, or simply curious about what support looks like, this list is offered as a starting place. It's not comprehensive. But it's sincere.

If the ritual of the pint has ever felt too heavy, these are the hands that reach back.

UNITED STATES

SAMHSA (Substance Abuse and Mental Health Services Administration)
National agency offering treatment locators, crisis helplines, and mental health support.
https://www.samhsa.gov

Alcoholics Anonymous (AA)
A worldwide peer-support fellowship offering local meetings, sponsorship, and recovery resources.
https://www.aa.org

Shatterproof
Nonprofit dedicated to ending addiction stigma and improving access to science-based treatment.
https://www.shatterproof.org

Faces & Voices of Recovery
National recovery advocacy organization working to support long-term healing and systems change.
https://facesandvoicesofrecovery.org

IRELAND

Alcohol Action Ireland
Independent advocacy group focused on reducing alcohol harm through research, policy, and public education.
https://alcoholactionireland.ie

Merchants Quay Ireland
Offers compassionate, nonjudgmental support for addiction, homelessness, and mental health—including detox and recovery services.
https://www.mqi.ie

Coolmine Therapeutic Community
Provides residential and community-based rehabilitation programs for individuals and families affected by addiction.
https://www.coolmine.ie

CORPORATE AWARENESS PLATFORMS

These programs are supported by Guinness's parent company, Diageo. They focus on moderation, education, and responsible drinking—not treatment.

DrinkIQ (Diageo)
Alcohol education tools, drink trackers, and resources for informed choices about alcohol.
https://www.drinkiq.com

Drinkaware Ireland
Independent charity focused on reducing alcohol misuse, supported in part by Diageo.
https://www.drinkaware.ie

Note: These corporate awareness platforms do not offer counseling or crisis intervention. If you need help now, please reach out to a recovery organization or medical professional.

MORE ONLINE

For updates to this list and additional resources, visit:

www.pintsandpower.com/alcohol-support

You're not alone. The stories in this book live in the same world as yours—where laughter and silence often share the same room. If today feels hard, reach out. There's no shame in asking for help. In fact, it may be the most Irish thing you can do.

Sláinte—whatever the glass holds.

Acknowledgments

A book like this is never written alone. It is poured out of stories shared, laughter carried, memories entrusted, and encouragement given along the way. What follows is less a list of thanks than a recognition of the people whose presence gave this work its shape.

Shuggy stands first among them — not just for the pints he pours, but for the space and spirit he's created at Boland's, a living room where this book could take root.

Michaela, Gareth, Kevin, Ged, and Barefoot Scott added their voices, their rituals, and their memories, proving that Guinness is never just a drink but a thread that binds people together.

Friendship leapt oceans through **Barry and Brigid**, whose hospitality and faith in this project reminded me that Irishness travels wherever hearts are open.

The music of **Niall Connelly and Danny O'Reilly** gave sound to the themes running beneath these pages and reminded me that song and story are kin.

My sister-in-law, **Kerrie**, deserves a place here too. She first crossed Ireland's shores with me back in college, and her passion for all things Irish — including the pint — helped light the fire of inspiration that would later burn into this book.

The staff at Boland's Bar and Patio welcomed me as one of their own: **Liv, John, Michaela, Liz, Conor, Casey, Lindsey, Dave, and Mike B.** Perfect pints and perfect nights are learned, but your generosity of spirit and kindness are the greatest gifts of all.

I'll be forever grateful to the amazing **Davy Holden** for encouraging me to dive fully into this idea, and for his historical perspective and experience that helped me understand the balance between passion and responsibility in my writing and research.

To the regulars, musicians, and friends on Water Street — **Bridie and Niamh, Kyra, Vinny, Anthony, Andy and Meghan, Kevin, Megan, Mustache Scott, Mike Ladd, Ashley, Jenn, Skip, Cait, Abraham, Sean, Shion and Christine, Mike M., Maureen, John, Bryant, Hailey, Nina, Chris, Gary , the crew from Bay State, and The Healy's — Don and Sheila** — and everyone else for whom space does not permit, it's been great sharing the living room with you each weekend. Here's to many more.

And, as always, my family — **Lisa, Katie, Tony, Elisabeth, and Caroline** — gave me the patience, love, and grounding without which no words would have been written.

This book is theirs as much as it is mine. May this acknowledgment serve not as an ending, but as a raised glass to each of them.

About the Author

Michael Villa is a husband, father of four, entrepreneur, amateur oil painter, and, almost by accident, an author. His deep connection to Ireland began as a family journey and grew into an enduring passion. As the founder and president of Dovetail Internet Technologies, LLC, he has spent decades building innovative solutions for businesses, but his heart has always been drawn to the people, history, and culture that inspire meaningful connection.

Pints and Power is his debut book, born from countless conversations, travels, and shared pints on both sides of the Atlantic. Through these pages, Mike has tried to capture the quiet, powerful ways a single brand has flowed beneath the story of a nation — and, perhaps, the story of each of us in some small way.

When he's not running his business, painting with an eye for realism and the shifting play of light, or tending the grill for a backyard BBQ, Mike can often be found enjoying live music, exploring Ireland's hidden corners, or sharing a pint and a good story with friends both old and new. He lives in Massachusetts with his family and makes frequent trips to Ireland, always in search of the next story beneath the foam.

FIRST POUR EDITION

REFERENCES

Audley, Fiona. 2024. *Former pub where Michael Collins convened intelligence unit meetings gets heritage plaque.* April 7. Accessed August 22, 2025. https://www.irishpost.com/history/former-pub-where-michael-collins-convened-intelligence-unit-meetings-gets-heritage-plaque-270603.

Blue News. 2025. *Guinness production is boosted.* Accessed May 31, 2025. https://www.bluewin.ch/en/news/guinness-production-is-boosted-2547244.html.

Boland, Margaret, and Thomas L. Rooney. 2009. *The Irish Pioneer: A Historical Novel of the Life of Tobias F. Boland.* Mobile, Alabama: Magnolia Mansions Press.

Bourke, Edward J. 2016. The Guinness Story: The Family. The Business. The Black Stuff. Dublin: The O'Brien Press Ltd.

Bunbury, Turtle. 2021. The Irish Diaspora: Tales of Emigration, Exlie and Imperialism. New York: Thames & Hudson, Ltd.

Connolly, Niall. n.d. *May 12th, 1916- A Song for James Connolly.* Accessed 15 2025, June. https://niallconnolly.bandcamp.com/track/may-12th-1916-a-song-for-james-connolly.

Connolly, Niall. 2016. *May 12th, 1916- A Song for James Connolly.* Performed by Glen Hansard and Niall Connolly. Live @ Coughlan's, Cork. December 20. Accessed June 15, 2025. https://www.youtube.com/watch?v=vbz74mGciXU.

2005. *Dublin Presented by Ronnie Drew.* DVD. Directed by Peter Galligan. Produced by Celtic Note Productions. Performed by Ronnie Drew.

Drinks Ireland. 2023. *Irish Beer Market Report.* Market Report, Dublin: Drinks Ireland IBEC.

Duff, Charles. 1966. *Six Days to Shake an Empire*. Cranbury, New Jersey: A. S. Barnes and Co., Inc.

Evans, Bryce. 2014. How Guinness Saved Ireland. June. Accessed August 22, 2025. https://www.irishamerica.com/2014/05/how-guinness-saved-ireland/.

Foley, Anthony. 2024. *Estimate of Alcohol Consumption per Adult in 2023*. Commissioned Report, Dublin: Drinks Industry Group of Ireland.

Foster, R. F. 2015. Vivid Faces: The Revolutionary Generation in Ireland 1890-1923. New York: W. W. Norton & Company.

Goldfarb, Aaron. 2023. *'We Don't Sell Stout. We Sell Guinness.' How One Irish Beer Became a Global Powerhouse*. May 23. Accessed August 24, 2025. https://www.wineenthusiast.com/culture/beer/guinness-beer-history.

Guinness Storehouse Ltd. 2023. *The Story of Guinness*. Accessed May 2025, 2025. https://www.guinness-storehouse.com/en/discover/story-of-guinness.

Guinness, Michele. 1989. The Guinness Legen: The Changing Fortunes of a Great Family. London: Hodder & Stoughton Ltd.

Guinness, Patrick. 2008. Arthur's Round: The Life and Times of Brewing Legend Arthur Guinness. London: Peter Owen Publishers.

Guinness, Rory. 2025. *World of Guinness*. London: Scala Arts & Heritage Publishers Ltd.

Holden, Davy. 2025. *Irish American History Workshop*. (hosted online). Accessed July 10, 2025.

Irish Around The World. 2021. *Top 10 Guinness Drinking Countries In The World*. Accessed May 31, 2025. https://irisharoundtheworld.com/top-10-guinness-drinking-countries.

Kate Curran, interview by Turtle Bunbury. 2023. *Sense of Flavour, Behind the Guinness Gates*. Audio Podcast. Accessed May 26, 2025. https://open.spotify.com/episode/73elK5vba1tvob9nlqAFe1.

Ladd, Mike. 2015. *Blackstone Cúil*. Comp. Mike Ladd. https://blackstonecuil.bandcamp.com/track/blackstone-c-il.

MacManus, Seumas. 1944. *The Story of the Irish Race.* 4th Revised Edition. New York: The Devin-Adair Company.

MarketScreener. 2025. *Diageo : Ireland The Home of Guinness.* Accessed 31 2025, May. https://www.marketscreener.com/quote/stock/DIAGEO-PLC-4000514/news/Diageo-Ireland-The-Home-of-Guinness-50014638.

McGowan, Ian. n.d. *Martin J. Sheridan: "A Peerless Athlete".* Accessed July 14, 2025. http://www.wingedfist.org/Sheridan_peerless_athlete.html.

Myers, Benjamin, and Graham Lees. 1997. *The Encyclopedia of World Beers: A Reference Guide for Connoisseurs.* Edison, NJ: Chartwell Books.

O'Brien, Flann. 1939. "The Workman's Friend." In *At Swim-Two-Birds.* London: Longmans, Green and Co.

Osburn, Christopher. 2025. *How to Split the G: The Unofficial Rules of Guinness Golf.* July 18. Accessed August 22, 2025. https://manofmany.com/culture/how-to-split-the-g-guinness.

Pepper, Barrie. 1996. The International Book of Beer: A Guide to the World's Most Popular Drink. New York: Robert M. Todd.

Radnedge, Aidan. 2024. *Revealed: The secret process to remove alcohol from Guinness 0.0... and why bosses say charging over £6 a pint for it is fair.* September 22. Accessed July 26, 2025. https://www.dailymail.co.uk/news/article-13879035/revealed-the-secret-process-to-remove-alcohol-from-guinness-00-and-why-bosses-say-charging-over-6-a-pint-for-it-is-fair.html.

Randall, Colin. 2024. *Christy Moore interviewed: A Terrible Beauty and a 'privileged life'.* October 31. Accessed July 26, 2025. https://www.salutlive.com/2024/10/christy-interview-will-do-it-up-for-posting-just-before-album-release-nov-1.html.

Reuters. 2024. *British, Irish PMs seek to reset strained ties over pints of Guinness.* July 17. Accessed May 24, 2025. https://www.reuters.com/world/uk/british-irish-pms-seek-reset-strained-ties-over-pints-guinness-2024-07-17.

Scottish License Trade News. 2023. *Stout wars – challengers battle for a bigger share of the dark side.* Accessed May 2023, 2025. https://sltn.co.uk/2023/12/02/stout-wars-new-challengers-battle-for-a-bigger-share-of-the-dark-side.

Sproule, Luke. 2024. *No Guinness shortages for Northern Ireland's pubs.* Accessed May 31, 2025. https://www.bbc.com/news/articles/ce90gl397evo.

Stanley, Isabelle. 2023. Shane MacGowan's life through quotes: 12 unforgettable one-liners from The Pogues rocker about drinking, women, and breaking into America. November 30. Accessed August 23, 2025. https://www.dailymail.co.uk/news/article-12809941/Shane-MacGowans-life-quotes-Pogues.html.

Sweeney, Tanya. 2021. *Colin Farrell: 'After 20 years of drinking the way I drank, the sober world is pretty scary'.* March 4. Accessed August 23, 2025. https://www.irishtimes.com/culture/film/colin-farrell-after-20-years-of-drinking-the-way-i-drank-the-sober-world-is-pretty-scary-1.4501552.

The Irish Post. 2022. *Irish Harp: did Ireland's national symbol come from Guinness?* June 9. Accessed May 25, 2025. https://www.irishpost.com/life-style/irish-harp-did-irelands-national-symbol-come-from-guinness-235523.

Trinity College Dublin. 2015. *The Long Room.* September. Accessed August 9, 2025. https://www.tcd.ie/library/old-library/long-room.

Vickery, Amanda. 1998. *The Gentleman's Daughter.* London: Yale University Press.

Writ in Water. 2015. *Kinda like a pint of Guinness.* 04 14. Accessed June 21, 2025. https://writ-in-water.com/2015/04/14/kinda-like-pint-guinness.

Yenne, Bill. 2007. *Guinness: The 250-Year Quest for the Perfect Pint.* Hoboken, New Jersey: John Wiley & Sons.

INDEX